THE ESSENTIAL
COCKATOO

Laurie Baker and Stuart Borden

3

Avian Publications
6380 Monroe St. NE
Minneapolis MN 55432

Bruce Burchett Publisher/Owner
www.avianpublications.com
bruce@avianpublications.com
Phone & fax 763-571-8902

National Library of Canada Cataloguing in Publication

Baker, Laurie / Borden, Stuart
The Essential Cockatoo / Laurie Baker and Stuart Borden

ISBN 0.910335-08-7
1. Parrots -- Cockatoo. 2. Parrots -- Training.
I. Title.

Production and Design

Silvio Mattacchione and Co. / Peter A. Graziano Limited
1251 Scugog Line 8, RR#1.
Port Perry, ON, Canada L9L 1B2
Telephone: 905.985.3555
Fax: 905.985.4005

silvio@silvio-co.com
graziano@andrewswireless.net
www.silvio-co.com

4

Photo by Michael Fink

About The Book

The *Essential Cockatoo* is co-authored by Laurie Baker, bird breeder and behaviorist and owner of the Feathered Follies bird shop in Lafayette, California; and Stuart Borden, a writer who acquired his first cockatoo, a Goffin's named Coco, at Laurie's establishment. Our focus is the selection, care and training of cockatoos as personal companions.

A cockatoo is no less wild and a good deal smarter than a Bengal tiger. Although keeping such a creature demands quick access to clear, expert advice, the typical bird care book is an outdated jumble of homespun tips and anecdotes. Our mission was to write something fun to read yet also thorough, specific to species and easy to use. We even include a section of forms and checklists to help manage your bird's health and progress.

Additionally, the book addresses some intriguing aspects of birds in general. After all, taxonomically speaking cockatoos are a single subspecies of a species of a genus of a subfamily of a family of an order of a class of a subphylum of a phylum of the Kingdom Animalia, and if you want to know a bird you have to meet her family, velociraptors and all.

Fun and practical, *The Essential Cockatoo* is the only book you need to select, train and nurture your new companion.

5

About The Authors

Laurie Baker owns the renowned Feathered Follies bird shop in Lafayette, California. Her education includes a B.A. from St. Mary's College, a Certificate in Ornithology from Cornell University and frequent updates on ornithology and related subjects through seminars at the University of California – Davis. Certified by the Pet Joint Advisory Council, she is a companion bird breeder and behaviorist and a recognized authority on rescue birds. Her writing has appeared in several avian publications. Currently she serves as a California State Coordinator for the American Federation of Aviculture.

Stuart Borden received his B.A. from Hofstra University and his Master of Fine Arts in Creative Writing from San Diego State University. His work includes fiction and non-fiction books, as well as articles, short stories, newsletters and translations. He is the proud owner, along with his wife, Ginger Russell, of a Goffin's cockatoo named Coco, who provided the inspiration for this handbook.

DIABLO

BEST
OF THE EAST BAY

Best Place To Get A Good Bird
Feathered Follies

Acknowledgments

Thanks first of all to Ginger Russell, who did the mock-up, collected photographs from around the world and prepared the graphics for submission, meanwhile handling her own, very demanding job. Thanks to Feathered Follies' manager Jeannie Landry for her digital photos, her constant good humor and her boundless competence.

Thanks to bird-loving photographers from South Africa to Australia whose works embellish these pages.

Thanks finally to the bright and beautiful cast, Abbie, Mickey, Indy and especially Coco.

Thanks to Dr. Brian Speer, who gave generously of his time not only to provide a forward for the book, but also to critique the original manuscript.

Foreword

Cockatoos, and birds in general, are almost magical creatures. We keep them in our homes for a variety of reasons--their beauty, their personalities, their mimicry. They brighten and enrich our lives. The amazing characteristics of cockatoos lend us insight into their nature and, on reflection, into our own. While keeping such birds can be challenging, our interactions and relationships with them present us with many, often mutual rewards.

As written by Stuart and Laurie *The Essential Cockatoo* helps clarify and articulate the manner in which one should keep a cockatoo in the home, sparing no punches about the hard work and diligence required in some areas. If it is true that an ounce of prevention is worth a pound of cure, *The Essential Cockatoo* will provide you with pounds of common-sense prevention and thought essential to the physical and behavioral well-being of your cockatoo. For both the current and the potential cockatoo owner, *The Essential Cockatoo* is a "must" addition to your reference shelf!

In addition to The Medical Center for Birds, his specialty clinical practice near San Francisco, Doctor Brian L. Speer, DVM, Dipl. ABVP (certified in avian practice), ECAMS (Certified specialist in Avian Medicine and Surgery - Europe), lectures and consults worldwide. He is co-author of The Large Macaws *and the highly popular* Birds for Dummies.

Contents

"Luke, I am your cockatoo"
Photo by Robert Tudor

Contents

A Cockatoo, You Say

Squaaaaaaaaaawk! In her cage next to me, Coco, a Goffin's cockatoo, wings splayed and tiara crest on display, lies on her back juggling a green-and-yellow jingle ball as big as she is and screeching at it like Bruce Lee. Squaaawk! Now, pausing, she eyes her foe and addresses it calmly, persuasively, Give it up, dude, you can't win (or to that effect; she's a California girl), only to flip onto her feet and heave it across the cage, screaming bloody murder as she hippity-hops in hot pursuit.

Catch!

With 150 channels on TV there's nothing quite as entertaining as Coco the Clown. But that's the reason for all those channels, isn't it? People like different things.

A cockatoo, you say.

Boasting 9,000 species, birds are Earth's largest and most diverse class of vertebrates, filling more ecological niches than mammals. Pigeons are to hawks as rabbits are to wolves. Big/small, smart/stupid, hunter/prey they resemble their wingless counterparts in myriad ways, including behavior. Some appeal to us more than others because of the very "human" or human-pleasing things they do. Canaries sing, parrots talk, cockatoos need; toucans adorn your home much like tropical fish. What you like (the species) and whom (the bird) depends on biological traits and individual personalities--yours and the bird's. Trust us, if you don't truly deeply love her you'll both be sorry. For all their lovableness, however, birds of any feather are very, very different from you and me. First off, most paleontologists agree they descend from dinosaurs, which separates them from us in ways we can't begin to understand. Second, there's a matter of perspective. We walk, they fly, so they see the world quite differently. Third, because humans are hunters (eyes in front for focus, a general fondness for meat, etc.) and most caged birds are prey (eyes at the side for wide-angle vision, a general fondness for nuts, seeds, fruits and vegetables, etc.), our notions, say, of danger, are also radically different. Fourth, cockatoos are creatures of the wild; unlike dogs and cats they've been bred as pets for a very short time, only a decade or so in many cases.

Consequently they have not developed a master-slave mentality or even much respect for human ways. You can't bend them to your will with shouts or punishment, or, practically speaking, persuade them to do what they don't want to do. In sum, man and bird are as different as, well, man and dinosaur.

So which dinosaur do you want to take home?

13

Once a dinosaur -
Illustrated by Natalie Love Adams —
Atalina's Creations

Always a dinosaur —
Photo by Feathered Follies

When dinosaurs fly.

The once outlaw theory that birds descend from dinosaurs, namely a group of bipedal hunters known as Microraptors, has become mainstream. Recently, Chinese paleontologists unearthed a pheasant-sized relative of Velociraptor (those smart little devils in *Jurassic Park*) called Dromaesaur, whose well-defined feathers are nearly identical to those of modern birds. Dubbed Microraptor gui (after Chinese paleontologist Gu Zhiwei) another raptor measured three feet long and came equipped with four feathered wings and a feathered tail. Then a team from New York's American Museum of Natural History discovered a five-foot-long Dilong doxous, the earliest known forbear of Tyrannosaurus rex, whose fossilized remains are imprinted with downy protofeathers.

Speaking of T-rex, a 70-million-year-old specimen found in Montana contains blood vessels similar to those of the modern ostrich. Indeed more than feathers tell us birds are dinosaurs. *Ornithomimid*, or "bird mimic," was a 7-foot tall, 15-foot long cousin of Velociraptor *and* Tyrannosaurus rex. Made of bone and keratin (the stuff of beaks, hair and claws) its huge bill was shaped like a duck's and like a duck's had a comb-like plate for straining food from water and sediment. *Rahona ostromi*, a raven-size critter with feathered wings, a long bony tail, opposable big toes for gripping and sickle-clawed second toes for hunting and defense, probably came from the group of dinosaurs known as advanced therapods. An ostrich-size carnivore called *Oviraptor* perched over its eggs in typical brooding position, suggesting that dinosaurs not only resembled birds but also behaved like them. Of no direct relation there was even a parrot-beaked dinosaur called *Psittacosaurid*. Put that in your cage and stroke it.

14

Canaries sing, parrots talk, cockatoos need. While they can be exceptionally vocal and even utter the occasional human word or phrase, cockatoos don't "talk" as fluently as, say, Amazons or African Grays. But that makes them no less intelligent. After all, who among us, even the smartest, can speak any of the 9,000 bird languages?

The word "cockatoo" derives from a Malaysian word meaning "cockatoo," a creature so unique it can't be described in terms of anything else. Her plumage is preponderantly of a single color, usually white, peach, gray or black, and comprises feathers that crumble into powder for grooming. Her wings are long, her tail stubby. To express her quirky personality she has a mobile crest that curves backward or forward, depending on species, and mobile cheek feathers to animate her face. So, yes, cockatoos are unique.

They do however come in diverse flavors. Which one's for you? Of the popular species, the neediest, often called "love sponges," are the Umbrella and the Moluccan, which also are among the largest. "Snuggle" is their middle name (unless they've been mistreated, or think they have, in which case "Biter,"

"Screamer" or "Feather Picker" may be more apt). Less snuggly are the smaller Goffin's and Bare-eyed cockatoos, a.k.a. "Houdini" and "Clown." You may need a padlock to keep your Goffin's in her cage--and don't make it a combination lock because she'll pick it. No kidding.

A cockatoo, you say.

Fair warning: it's like adopting a child (a frequent analogy) and what you don't know can hurt you both. Unlike children, moreover, cockatoos never grow up. Accordingly we've modeled our opus on Dr. Benjamin Spock's alternately famous and infamous child-rearing book, providing a clear, frank explanation of essentials as well as handy tips from veteran bird handlers, all to make life easier and more rewarding for you and your new feathered folly.

Who taught whom to talk?

Instead of a larnynx your bird has a syrinx, a group of thin vibrating muscles located near the base of her windpipe, so that try as she may she can never precisely mimic human words. But hold on: who's mimicking whom? Comparing the pitch profiles, or melodic shifts, of hundreds of bird songs to thousands of pop and classical melodies, Prof. Graham Pont, a musical analyst at Australia's University of New South Wales, has found them to be nearly identical. He infers that a bird-like "melodic skeleton" has prevailed throughout musical history. The image of St. Francis preaching to the birds, says he, reflects the shamanistic tradition "that if you are really intelligent you could understand bird language. It's a mythical memory of a historical fact that we did talk to the birds--that we learned language from them. [Language] could have been a...quick technological transfer by imitation."

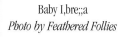

Baby I,bre;;a
Photo by Feathered Follies

Cast of Characters

Coco, also known as "Duchess of Whinger," "Puff Birdie," "B.B. (Busy Beak) Queen" and "Little Big Shot," is a four-year-old Goffin's who lectures at length on a variety of subjects in both English and a language all her own. She also plays bells, scarfs up popcorn, picks cage locks, de-beads her abacus (so she won't have to count so high?), splinters clothespins, upends bowls, shreds paper, performs acrobatics (Cirque de Soleil should be so good) and refuses to go to bed without a cuddle.

Abbie —
Photo by Feathered Follies

Having lived in the same home since chickhood, *Abbie*, an 11-year-old Umbrella, is trusting and exceptionally well-behaved. For a cockatoo. Though she loves to frolic outside her cage and cuddle and play with (nearly) anyone willing, she's picky about her food, especially its color, tossing the red pellets every whichaway to get at the green ones. And while in the morning she's relatively quiet, at dusk she spreads her crest, flaps her wings and shrieks with abandon for a good quarter-hour. She's a teaser, too, always stirring up trouble among the other birds (there are several in her household) and standing back to watch the fun.

Coco —
Photo by Ginger Russell

Mickey –
Photo by Feathered Follies

Mickey, a 14-year old Moluccan, is spectacular, both in appearance (two feet long with peachy-white feathering and a rust-colored crest) and in personality. If there's anything he likes better than playing (mind you, this is a bird that goes out for passes in cockatoo football) it's chewing and shredding. Cardboard boxes are good, and kids' toys, and cell phones. A clever lad, he'll dip water from his bowl with a bottle cap, tilt back his head and down it like a shot of rye. Vocabulary? Not bad, if you ignore meaning. Though meaning, of course, isn't Mickey's goal; what Mickey's after is the sound of his own voice, the louder the better, at any hour of day or night. Unlike most cockies he loves kids. Grown-ups, however, had better behave.

Indy –
Photo by Feathered Follies

Indy, a 5-year-old Lesser Sulphur-Crested, is now in his second home. He's not a biter. He's not a screamer. He's not even a feather picker. Because of his nervous temperament, however, he requires more patience and TLC than the average family can muster. An active, playful bird, he loves to hop on his bungee and yell and flap until he sets it spinning. He's fond of cuddling (and being only 13 inches long fits nicely under a jacket); he has a favorite person (yet will go to anyone who gains his trust); and while he's a poor speech mimic he's a great communicator, using his own language, vocal, facial and physical, to get his point across.

Choosing Your Cockatoo

Other issues

Coco, Goffin's Cockatoo
Photo by Ginger Russell

Got my eye on you

WHY A COCKATOO?

They're smart, cute, fun, cuddly and loyal, all of which makes them great companions.

WHY NOT A COCKATOO?

Responsibility. You'll learn soon enough that a cockatoo is not your ordinary pet. You can leave your cat some extra food, water and litter and go away for the weekend. Not so your cockatoo. You can feed your dog dry food or canned food or both and consider it reasonably well nourished. Not so your cockatoo. You can punish your cat or dog and mend its ways. Not so your cockatoo. You can figure, realistically, that your cat really isn't bothered by your marital spats. Not so your cockatoo. You can even ignore your cat or dog most of the time to no obvious ill effect. Not so your cockatoo. Not by any means.

Cockatoos are emotional, intelligent, fragile beings; you can ruin them psychologically and/or physically in short order. Indeed, nurturing a cockatoo is right up there with nurturing a human child, and demands of you a level of commitment that definitely has an impact on your life. For instance, who'll care for the bird when you travel? We've all seen the nanny movies: inexperienced sitters are risky at best. Or maybe she's ill or having serious behavioral problems, such as feather picking. Unlike most animals, moreover, she may live upward of seventy years. Who'll adopt her if she survives you? And is that *lucky* person ready, willing and able to assume the responsibility? In a nutshell, be sure you're up to the job before taking it on.

Cost. Besides the bird, who doesn't come cheap, there's the cage, the toys, the gym, the toys, the T-stand, the toys, the feeding dishes, the toys, the accessories, the toys, the veterinarian, the toys, the baby-sitter, the toys, the food (pellets, seed, snacks, fruit, nuts and veggies), the toys, and more of the same in perpetuity.

Neediness. They're gluttons for attention.

Powder down and allergies. The white varieties especially produce a great deal of powder down. It settles like dust and you may be allergic. While there are things you can do to offset it there's absolutely nothing you can do to stop it.

Noise. With voices to call across broad expanses of jungle, cockatoos can be loud--ear-splitting is a common description--often at sunrise, usually at sunset, and a time or two during the day for good meas-

20

ure (see Section 5, Understanding your cockatoo, and Section 6, Training your cockatoo). Some, notably the Goffin's, even scream in the dark, which can be unnerving. Noisiest are the Umbrellas, the Moluccans and the Greater Sulphurs.

Bonding. A cockatoo may bond with an individual person to the extent that separation is traumatic and she becomes jealous of others. Proper socialization is the only known cure.

Destructiveness. A happy cockatoo is forever exploring and testing with her beak. In other words, if you let her, your bird will attempt to take apart or chew (absent the baby drool) anything she comes in contact with. Even the smaller species wield powerful beaks and are always in search of something gnawable. Forget plastic dishes and flimsy cage bars, and above all watch your fingers until she's trained. Her beak has three sharp points of contact, one on the upper mandible and two on the lower, which also has a chisel edge. In other words, she can puncture you in three places and slash you at the same time.

Messiness. Collective nouns for birds include: an exaltation of larks, a parliament of owls, a tiding of magpies, a cast of hawks, a building of rooks, a nye of pheasants, a charm of finches, a

Listen up, mates, we left some leaves down there!
– *Photo by Michael Fink*

21

party of jays, a siege of herons, a mustering of storks, a wedge of swans, a spring of teal, an ostentation of peacocks, a descent of woodpeckers and a murder of crows.

For cockatoos we've coined the term "mess," which may consist of a single member. Really, you won't believe the mess a single cockatoo can make. Tossing food from bowls. Tossing the bowls. Shredding newspaper into parade confetti. Scattering the splinters of whatever's left of the wood within reach. And in this respect size means nothing: what a Bare-eyed lacks in stature it more than makes up for in energy.

CHOOSING THE RIGHT SPECIES

About 300 of the world's 9,000 bird species are parrots and of these only 17 are cockatoos (excluding the cockatiel). Ranging in size and mien from the foot-long, subtly hued Goffin's to the huge, spectacular black palm, they originate exclusively in or near Australia, New Guinea and Indonesia (see Appendix). While their life cycles are similar to that of humans they reach sexual maturity at between two and five years of age. All have conspicuous gray, white, blue or purple rings around the eyes. All have

Blowin' in the wind –
Photo by Andy Cranston

22

A cockatoo mess
Photo by Michael Fink

A mess of cockatoos
Photo by Michael Fink

crests. All have bald spots beneath their crests. All have short bobbed tails. All have powder down to insulate the body and clean and waterproof the outer plumage. If not renowned as talkers (human speech) they can certainly talk, the Bare-eyed species particularly.

Cockatoos vary greatly in personality from bird to bird. Emotionally they resemble children and love attention, which they'll do almost anything to attract. Like kids too they are unabashedly self-centered and prone to jealousy. Worse, they never grow out of the so-called "gimme" stage, which by and large makes them undesirable as children's pets. (Rule of thumb: never leave a child alone with a cockatoo.)

Exceptionally intelligent, cockatoos not only understand complex human instructions but also learn tricks through classic modeling behavior (watching and imitating other birds) and experiments of their own device. What's more they possess excellent memory both short- and long-term; once met you're remembered with all your warts. While as a rule steady and adaptable, they may, like

23

any intelligent animal, suffer mood extremes. Abused or neglected birds even have nervous breakdowns.

Moluccan Cockatoo
Photo by Everett Butler

Large species

• *Moluccan or Salmon-Crested Cockatoo (Cacatua moluccensis).* The Moluccan Cockatoo is white in color with a salmon blush over-all and a deeper salmon in his crest. Native to the coastal forests of the Moluccan Islands, he's nearly two feet long, wields a large and potentially destructive beak and can be (okay, is) rau-cous, in particular at sunrise and sunset. Like the Goffin's he may occasionally scream in the dark. Also he produces lots and lots of feather powder. Also, too, he's high-strung as a racehorse, which makes him the perfect candidate for screaming and feather picking. So much for the cons. As for the pros, he's playful, gorgeous and makes a great companion. Just be sure you have lots of room, a good vacuum cleaner and tolerant neighbors.

Umbrella Cockatoo
Photo by Stacey Hoth

• *Umbrella or White-Crested Cockatoo (Cacatua alba).* Known to fans as Aumbie@ the Umbrella cockatoo also hails from the Moluccan Islands. About eighteen inches long, she's white in color with yellow feathering under her wings, and derives the name Umbrella from her spreading crest. Like the Moluccan she can be loud,

24

destructive and cuddly to a fault. Spoil or mistreat her and pay the price. She may also, like the Goffin's, have a toe fetish and gleefully chase your little piggies till you go wee-wee-wee. Our advice: wear shoes.

(From right to left)

Lesser Sulphur Crested Cockatoo, Mediium Sulphur Crested Cockatoo (Eleanora), Greater Sulphur Crested Cockatoo

Photo by Everett Butler

• *Greater Sulphur-Crested Cockatoo (Cacatua Galerita).* The Greater Sulphur-Crested inhabits the swamps and forests of Australia, Tasmania, King Island, New Guinea and Aru Island. Measuring twenty inches long, he's mostly white with yellow shading on the undersides of his wing and tail feathers and a bright yellow crest like a spiked hairdo. Island species include the Eleanora and the Triton. Although fun and easy to train the Galerita has an uneven temperament and is notorious for biting, chewing and screaming.

• *Eleanora Cockatoo (Cacatua Galerita Eleanora).* The Eleanora, or "medium sulphur-crested cockatoo," hails from the Aru Islands west of New Guinea. At about 18 inches long with white plumage, pale yellow ear coverts and yellow shading under her wings and tail, she is similar in behavior and appearance to the Greater Sulphur-Crested.

Small(er) species

• *Lesser Sulphur-Crested Cockatoo (Cacatua sulphurea).* Indigenous to the open forests of Butung and the Celebes, the Lesser Sulphur Crested is roughly fourteen inches long and similar in coloring to the Eleanora and the Greater Sulphur Crested. A screamer. Tends to be nervous and shy. Older males particularly are notorious for biting.

• *Citron-Crested Cockatoo (Cacatua sulphurea citrinocristata).* A subspecies of the Lesser Sulphur-Crested, the Citron-Crested is much the same in size and appearance except for her bright-orange crest and orange-shaded ear

25

Citron Crested Cockatoo
Photo by Everett Butler

peramental and prone to form strong, erratic bonds that lead to bad habits. A good talker, but not so hot at pronunciation. She may scream in the dark (at the honk of a horn, the cough of a loved one, a whim or during sex), chase your toes obsessively and open every lock you devise for her cage. She may also pick her feathers, shred your couch and use her beak to get her way, then arbitrarily change her mind about whom she loves best. But when she isn't driving you nuts she will, guaranteed, bring you joy and laughter.

coverts. Known as a prankster and favored by cockatoo aficiona-dos, the Citron is native to Sumba, an island located south of the Celebes and west of Timor.

Goffin's
Cockatoo

• *Goffin's Cockatoo (Cacatua Goffini).* Former habitat: the dimunitive islands of Tanimbar, off the coast of New Guinea. About a foot long, the Goffin's is white with peach blush about her head, neck and breast, and yellow shading beneath her wings and tail. Her crest is small but highly expressive. Bright, wild-at-heart and hyperactive, she's easily bored, as well as reactionary, tem-

• *Bare-eyed Cockatoo or Little Corella (Cacatua sanguinea).* Distributed mainly throughout the dry inland areas of eastern, northern and northwestern Australia (there is also a New Guinea sub-species) the Little Corella is considered a pest and treated as such, rather cruelly, by local farmers. Except for his size--about 16 inches long and a little stocky--and the gray featherless eye rings from which he derives his "bare-eyed" name, he closely resembles the Goffin's. One of the most intelligent parrots, he's a great clown and the best talker of the cockatoos, quickly learning to mimic words in a very loud voice. He's also a chewer and tends to obesity, so protect

Bare Eyed Cockatoo
Photo by Everett Butler

Rose Breasted Cockatoo
Photo by Michael Fink

your furniture and limit the seeds in his fare. Beware too his tendency to emotionally "overload" and start nipping. Read the signs and save a finger.

• *Galah or Rose-breasted Cockatoo (Eolophus roseicapillus).* "Rosie" the Galah inhabits the dry areas, parks and farmlands of most of the Australian interior, and like the Bare-eyeds and Sulphur-cresteds is considered a pest by local farmers, who slaughter her kind by the thousands. About 14 inches long with a rose-tinged head and lower body, she has soft gray wings and a matching back and a stubby, pink-to-white crest. She's a pretty good talker, too, with a distinctive

voice, and like the Goffin's comes charged with energy. She also shares the Goffin's knack for picking locks. While gentler and quieter than most cockies she's very cautious, with a strong fear-and-flight response. Take it slow and keep her wings trimmed.

CHOOSING THE RIGHT BIRD

Captured wild or raised in captivity? Smuggling is cruel in ways you don't want to hear about at bedtime. It also kills an inordinate number of birds and in some cases may already have extinguished entire species. Conscience tells you anyway not to take creatures from the wild. As to whether birds should be bred in captivity, it's a moot question: what's done

27

is done. Moreover, some species, such as the Goffin's (whose home islands have been severely deforested for lumber and subsistence farming), might be extinct without domestic breeding programs. No cockatoos have been imported legally to the United States since the Wild Bird Conservation Act of 1992. All babies sold legally since then were hatched in captivity, resulting in better quality and availability of kept birds. While loss of habitat kills more birds than domestic breeding could ever save, such programs have paradoxically allowed more wild birds to remain free.

Young or old?

The baby bird. It's best to acquire a newborn that will be hand-fed and weaned at the shop while you go about bonding with her and learning the ropes. Such a process insures not only good nutrition and professional care for the chick, but just as importantly a high degree of socialization: physical handling, finger ("step-up") training, interaction with caring human beings. Truth is, the cockatoo who is reared by her parents and simultaneously socialized by people will be every bit as tame as a hand-fed bird, and perhaps better adjusted.

A cautionary note: young

A few more weeks is all I ask
Photo by Feathered Follies

is better only up to a point. Don't let anyone sell you an unweaned bird; nurturing such a frail, helpless creature is fraught with peril.

The mature bird. Nobody knows for sure how long cockatoos live, even in captivity: they've been popular as companions for only two or three decades, so zoo statistics and anecdotal evidence is about all we have to go on. Fifty to seventy years is a good guess. Because the bird is caged, though, she's probably under-exercised, over-fed and at least mildly neurotic, which together will produce signs of aging long before her three-score-and-ten: heart ailments, arthritis, hypertension, cataracts. No anthropomorphism intended. Well, maybe a little. Like people, moreover, senior cockatoos get set in their often irksome ways. That an adult bird is available at all arouses suspicion; ask why she's available and keep

28

asking until you get a straight answer. If there are major health or behavioral issues (or if you *can't* get a straight answer) walk away. All too often parrots are recycled for problems that get worse after every round. As much as you may pity them, most such birds are not for amateurs; only experienced caregivers should apply.

Don't get us wrong, there are some great adults out there. Usually quieter than youngsters, they may also exhibit more emotional subtlety and ability to communicate. Just consider what you're taking on. Giving a mature bird a home is laudable, but is your home the right one?

The rescue bird. If adopting a mature bird is problematic, adopting a rescue bird is downright risky. To start with, rescue is the operative word. Along the way something's gone wrong, with the owner, with the bird, even with the law (i.e., smuggling) and any of these reasons may have damaged the health and/or emotional stability of the cockatoo in need of rescue. In other words, our precautions regarding older birds apply to rescue birds in spades. Before adopting do proper diligence and steel yourself to the possible consequences. We know it's easy to say, but don't let

price (from free to "cheap" to "reasonable") be the determining factor.

If you don't choose a weanling, spend time with the bird and build a profile: history, bad habits, health. Before the age of sexual maturity is usually best. Above all don't adopt on impulse. Trust us: it's like adopting ET, so there's a lot to consider before taking her home.

Soulmates
Photo by Everett Butler

Male or female? Overall, adult males may be a bit larger and/or more aggressive than females and supposedly have fewer medical problems, but in terms of intelligence and personality both genders make good companions. The sex of most

29

adult cockatoos can be determined by eye color (solid black for males, reddish brown for females), while in some black species feather coloring tells the tale. If you really want to be sure, though, get the bird DNA-sexed. (See below.)

Small or large? Size counts. A tiger is not a house cat, a wolf is not a chihuahua and a marlin is not a guppy. So too a Moluccan cockatoo is not a Goffin's.

Multiple cockatoos? We strongly suggest you start with one. Otherwise see Section 2, Taking your cockatoo home, and inset this page. Also refer to Further Reading.

WHERE TO "ADOPT" A COCKATOO

Retailers. First-timers should stick to reputable retailers. Consult veterinarians, the Better Business Bureau, the local parrot association, etc. Visit the store several times to observe. Is it clean? (Use your nose as well as your eyes.) Do the birds have enough cage room to spread their wings? Do they look healthy and alert? Do they have fresh water and pelletized food? Are they groomed and boarded separately from other animals, where access can be controlled and infection prevent-

Two of a kind.

Paired cockatoos are usually less tame and trainable than single birds but on the other hand require considerably less human attention. By all means choose opposite sexes. Let them observe each other from well separated cages for a few weeks, then bring the cages together on neutral ground. Signs of compatibility include crest erection and tail fanning. If all goes well try placing them in the same cage; if not, repeat the process another day. Continued failure signals a need to rethink your matchmaking.

CAUTION: If you want to breed cockatoos we suggest you change your mind. It's a risky, complicated business even for experienced breeders. It's also dangerous; in breeding season captive cockatoos frequently assault each other with ugly results.

ed? Are visitors to the nursery asked to wash their hands before touching the birds? Do the staff know and show interest in birds? (Do they ask *you* a lot of questions? If so, good; if not, they may not know or care enough to do so.) Do they handle birds with compassion and competence? Check the shelves for toys, perches, pelletized diets, *current* reference books.

Breeders. Often a less personal experience, allowing little one-on-one interaction for bonding, etc. Generally, though, the checklist for breeders is the same as for retailers.

Rescue organizations. Often rescue birds have been ill-treated and so, for the novice, may be hard to handle. (See above and list, Appendix.)

Newspaper advertisements. Buyer beware.

ADOPTER'S CHECKLIST

(See Section 7. Forms, checklists and records.)

You have the right, indeed the obligation, to examine your cockatoo before taking her home. A stitch in time, et cetera. In general, avoid the bird who fluffs up and keeps his head under his wing; he may be sick. He should be alert, perch comfortably and move smoothly and efficiently. His body should be well-muscled and of appropriate weight (feel the breast meat) with no signs of obesity. He should have no lumps, bumps or lesions. His breathing should be slow and even. He should step up and down without panic, refrain from biting, and stay when you touch him: fearless birds are consistently the most gentle. Ask about his parents, health, diet, behavior and so forth. Especially inquire if he's been well socialized. Take special heed of the following (see Section 5: Keeping your cockatoo healthy, for illustrations of cockatoo anatomy.)

Eyes. Clear, bright and alert. No bumps, lumps or scratches on eye rings; no discharge. A baby's eyes will be black.

Nasal openings. Clean and open; round and regularly shaped; should not extend into beak matter; no sign of irritation, no discharge (staining of feathers above the nostrils).

Beak. Fits together evenly with the upper mandible neatly closing over the lower; no signs of extensive wear; no white or yellow spots. Upper mandible should not be overgrown. A baby's beak must be soft and pliable.

Wings and plumage. Adults should be fully feathered. No evidence of lumps or bumps at base of wing feathers. Assure that wings are properly clipped (see illustration Section 4: Nurturing your cockatoo). Neither wing should droop and both should be held snugly to body. Overall plumage should be smooth with no bare patches (careful not to adopt a feather picker; see Section 3. Understanding your cockatoo, and Section 6. Keeping your cockatoo healthy). Babies may have few feathers but when the plumage is grown in it should be uniform. If the feathers are not yet opened look for sharply pointed spikes rather than rounded, unopened feathers, which

31

may indicate incurable beak-and-feather disease. A healthy, fully-weaned cockatoo will have powder on her plumage; rubbing the flight (largest) feathers should leave a slick residue on your fingers.

Legs. Equal thickness, scales smooth; no bumps, cuts or sores; no white or yellow spots.

Feet. Four toes to a foot, two to the front and two to the rear, each with its claw. (This arrangement of opposing toes is called zygodactyl; common only to parrots and woodpeckers, it allows the feet to double as hands.) Feet should have equal gripping strength and be equally warm (one warm and one cold may indicate a problem). Scales must be smooth with no yellow or white spots. Claws must not be overgrown.

Vent. Clean and free of soiling; not distended.

Droppings. Should have form and contain both white and dark-green matter. Though other colors may derive from something the bird has just eaten (blueberries) they may symptomize a problem. Birds excrete liquids and solids simultaneously so urine may be present. Watery droppings are typical of birds on formula, but in weaned birds consistently watery droppings suggest poor health.

32

Oops!

Behavior. Excessively noisy begging or obvious fear may be a sign of behavioral problems in hand-fed baby cockatoos.

Max grew his feathers back due to a healthy diet.

Photo by Feathered Follies

OTHER ISSUES

The sales contract. Some states require that the sale of a parrot be documented and reported. At a minimum, the contract should specify:

- Date of purchase
- Terms of sale and price paid
- Hatch date
- Species and gender (result of DNA test)
- Identification band and/or microchip number
- Polyoma vaccination date(s)
- Take-home weight

In addition, your contract should detail health guarantees, recommend a veterinary examination within two weeks, and stipulate action should the bird prove to be ill or have a pre-existing condition. An exchange rather than a refund is usually the remedy for serious problems.

Sex determination. In most cockatoos eye color is a poor way to determine gender. Likewise plumage. With regard to tests, surgical sexing is reliable, but easiest and most reliable is DNA sampling. Often this is arranged by your retailer. If not, ask your veterinarian.

Banding and microchip identification. Either or both. Preferably both.

For microchip tracking, call American Kennel Club Companion Animal Recovery at (800)252-7894. For traceable bird bands, contact the American Federation of Aviculture: Telephone: (512)585-9000, Website: http://www.afabirds.org, E-mail: afaoffice@earthlink.net.

The identification band should fit snugly enough to stay on but not so snugly as to harm the bird's ankle (or so loosely as to catch on something)

33

2

Taking Your Cockatoo Home

Say what?

THE CALL OF THE WILD

Even if bred and raised in captivity, cockatoos are, to repeat, wild animals, so when you bring one into your home you're bringing along her need for a wild environment: lots of room, lots of variety, lots of care and attention from her new, featherless flock mates.

As human beings we struggle against the encroaching chaos. We like things clean, quiet and organized. Cockatoos to the contrary thrive on disorder. What's a little mess in such a great big world? Anyhow that's what ants and worms and rodents are for, right? to clean things up. No wonder such creatures adapt reluctantly to the dimensions of human life,

regardless of cage size and quantity of toys: you just can't reduce the jungle or the outback to a corner of your family room.

Yet to keep a healthy bird you have to try.

Quick-witted and high-strung, your cockatoo doesn't like the inside of a cage any more than you would, and probably a good deal less. She has wings, remember, she can *fly*. Imagine being abducted at birth by aliens and taken to Mars as a pet. You don't know *what* you are, let alone *who*. You can't speak *your* language let alone *theirs*. You're fed foul-tasting pellets, watered through a tube and locked in a cage with a couple of boring toys for life. Worst of all you're never allowed to do what you were born to do: take to the heavens.

On the other hand don't expect a reward for leniency. If you're determined to give your cockatoo freedom to roam, prepare your house in keeping with Murphy's dictum that what can go wrong will. Toilet lids down, fish bowls covered, sinks drained (it doesn't take much water to drown a frantic bird); electrical cords concealed and/or armored; jewelry put away; kitchen access restricted, especially the stove, especially if it's gas, et cetera and so forth. Then pray.

35

Cockatoos are poor eaters (but first-rate wasters; testing, tossing and playing with food is a kick) particularly when the surroundings or the people or your clothes are new, or there are too many (pick your color) pellets in the mix, or it's Thursday afternoon or Saturday morning or February 29 or sunny or rainy or she'd rather play ball or be in Borneo. Also they're pickier than most parrots. Introduce new foods gradually, experimenting with preferences as you go. All intelligent beings, especially cockatoos, fear changes that are sudden or beyond their control. Let her participate. And be patient: the first no is seldom a final answer.

She may fast a while after going home. Hey, moving is stressful; give her a chance to acclimatize. If by the second or third day she hasn't come around, however, consult your vet. Stubborn cockatoos can starve themselves to death.

THE CAGE

Location. Set up the bird's cage in a quiet place in sight of human activity, such as the family room, thus allowing her to be involved but also enjoy her privacy. Don't make her home a stage. Similarly, place the cage in a corner or against a wall so all four sides aren't exposed. If

possible, place her main perch at about your chest height; too high may evoke notions of independence ("You talkin' to *me*?"), too low just the opposite, making her nervous and prone to self-defensive behavior.

Remember that cockatoos are native to hot climates. In captivity they use energy to keep warm that should be used for essential body functions. Keep the cage area at a temperature to which your bird is accustomed, but no lower, say, than the low 70s F (20s C). Keep the cage away from:

- Heating or air conditioning vents
- Doors, windows, drafts (especially in cold climates)
- Avenues of escape (doors, open windows, etc.)
- The kitchen with its potentially deadly fumes
- Direct sunlight

Shape. Avoid tall, round cages; cockatoos aren't helicopters.

Size. The largest practical, and at least one size up from that specified by the manufacturer, which is always minimum. In fact even small cockatoos ought to have macaw-size cages. There should be enough uncluttered space for the bird to flap her wings without touching the sides.

36

Le cage complet.

Make it fun but unclut-
tered. Layer it like a tree
but never place feeding
bowls beneath perches.
Using the top as a play
area is optional]

General construction.

• *Metal, not wood or plastic.* If the metal is galvanized make sure it's electroplated, not dipped.

• *Powder coating is best.* Avoid flaked or chipping paint.

• *Built to last.* Check welds, seams, nuts and bolts.

• *Bars.* Strong enough to resist bending; this is not a canary you're dealing with. Horizontal on two sides for climbing and spaced close so the bird won't get her head caught.

• *Watch for traps* that may catch wings, claws or heads.

• *Door.* Your bird must be able to enter and exit without lowering her crest. You must be able to work through the opening with both hands. Secure with a cockatoo-proof lock.

CAUTION: avoid guillotine doors.

• *Ornamentation.* None. You don't want to clean that filigree.

• *Poop tray.* A pull-out tray below the cage grill. Make sure there's enough distance between the grill and the bottom of the tray to prevent access; otherwise the bird will be pulling up and chewing soiled newspaper and discarded food.

• *Mess catcher.* An inverted metal skirt around the bottom of the cage helps catch the mess.

Set-up.

• *Bowls, dishes and bottles.* Use separate bowls for wet and dry foods and place them where they won't get too dirty too fast (worst place of all is beneath a perch). Choose ceramic or stainless steel. Inexpensive Pyrex-type bowls (sized according to bird) are great for treats, fruits, etc. Buy two sets of everything, keeping one in the dishwasher and one in the cage. Should you use a water bottle keep it clean and the water fresh; also check daily that the dispenser is working properly.

• *Cage liner.* Use newspaper; its ink retards bacteria, fungus and mold.

• *Perches.* Suggested diameter is one to two inches depending on the size of the bird. Supply perches of various shapes and diameters (think tree) to avoid cramping those zygodactyls into one grip size. Natural wood perches are preferable because they afford a better grip and also offer chewing material. Rope perches are good, too, and like the wooden variety can be tossed in the dishwasher. The sanded perches supplied with most cages are slippery, and while flexible bandage may ameliorate that problem it quickly becomes a slimy, germ-ridden mess. Sanded perches make good dowels--which, basically, they are--or, for the carpentry-challenged, kindling.

A mineral or concrete perch (*not* sandpaper) helps keep her nails blunt and her beak clean. Assure that all perches are properly fastened.

OTHER EQUIPMENT AND SUPPLIES

Time-out/travel/sleeping cage.
Large enough to accommodate her comfortably yet small enough to call portable and mean it. There are good collapsible cages on the mar-

Life on the lam
Photo by Robert Tudor

ket. Use it when the bird's getting on your nerves, or for travel, or as a sleeping cage. Test strength and spacing of bars.

Carrier. A dog or cat carrier also works as a travel cage. Buy the type with metal windows; plastic won't last. For trips, choose something roomy enough to accommo-

The Fugitive.

She's gone. Gone. If only you'd used a padlock. If only you hadn't yelled at her. If only you'd given her that peanut. If only... Then you recall the close calls you helped her avert all those years (the scalding coffee, the pearl earring, the Hershey bar) and start fretting about the perils she faces now, alone in the Cold Cruel World. Will she nibble on a redwood or a holly bush and keel over dead? or become lunch for a hawk's brood? or be felled by some imbecilic human with a rifle and an urge to use it?

Yet if many escaped parrots succumb to these hazards, others thrive in the great civilized outdoors, especially if enough of their feather have escaped to flock together. Take the conures of San Francisco: for years at his home on Telegraph Hill, Mark Bittner fed and cared for a growing flock of feral-to-wild cherryheads. (Check out his recent book, The Wild Parrots of Telegraph Hill; there's also a film documentary.) Or the Monk (Quaker) parrots of Brooklyn: built on high-voltage lines, their trulli-like, multi-unit co-ops occasionally catch fire and cause blackouts, inciting the city power company to raze the nests chicks and all. Then a rumor about psittacosis prompted New York State to launch a Monk-eradication campaign. Forgetaboutit. Not even East Coast winters faze the Monks; natives of Argentina, where the climate's not always temperate, they've taken over Flatbush like a rooftop mafia. The moral: if parrots can make it in Brooklyn they can make it anywhere, Chicago, Miami, Austin, psitticine fugitives squawking triumphantly across America. There are even reports of a cockatoo flock, sulphur-cresteds mainly, forming among the bucolic hills and inlets of Benicia in that never-never land twixt Napa and San Francisco. So don't let your crest fall if your Umbie takes wing. She's smart. She's tough. She's resourceful. And at least there aren't mobs of Australian farmers chasing her with shotguns. With a little luck she'll do just fine.

date a perch, cutting the perch to fit and screwing it on through opposite walls of the carrier a couple inches above the floor.

Bathing bowl/spray bottle. Cockatoos bathe frequently to control feather dust. Shower her once or twice a week, shampoo her once a month, and every day or so either mist her with a spray bottle and/or provide a shallow 12-to-14 inch flower-pot saucer so she can perform her own ablutions.

Humidifier. If your home is artificially heated and/or cooled most of the time, procure a heavy-duty cool-air humidifier, set it at 55-60 percent, and place it permanently near the bird's cage.

Exercise equipment. Chains, climbing ropes and such provide exercise, entertainment and maintenance of beak and claws.

Toys. Keep your bird supplied with a variety of interesting toys, as well as chewables, shreddables and feather substi-

40 tutes. She's smart and active; keep her challenged or she'll get bored and form bad habits. Beware toys she can break into small parts (say, a small bell with a fragile clapper) and accidentally swallow. Choose sizes appropriate to the size of the bird. For connectors, use

C-clamps, quicklinks or pear fasteners (stainless steel; other metals may be toxic when chewed) or even a leather strip if you don't mind tying it repeatedly. Should the toy come with a flimsy fastener, discard it (the fastener, not the toy) and replace it with any of the above. Limit the number of toys in her cage. Too much choice

Part of the toy selection at
Feathered Follies, Lafayette CA

both confuses and clutters, taking up room needed for flapping and climbing. Insofar as possible place toys just above perch level.

T-stand. A must for training, bathing, etc.

Gym or climbing tree. Either or both of these provides a taste of freedom and encourages exercise with a minimum of mess. An open perch atop the cage is better than nothing but limits creative activity. Note: as your cockatoo grows up she'll lose her baby caution and start getting off the gym, at which point staying on it becomes learned behavior.

Air filter. Cockatoos produce a lot of powder, so you may want to use an air filter, especially if you're prone to allergies.

Full-spectrum lighting. Outdoor birds need outdoor light. If your bird gets too little of it (light filtered through window glass is inadequate) try any of a variety of full-spectrum lamps available through bird and lighting retailers.

Hand vacuum. Need we explain?

Chair mats to protect the carpet under her cage and gym or climbing tree. Also available are plastic sheets that adhere to any floor surface and can be wiped clean or vacuumed. On uncarpeted floors we suggest newspaper: roll it up and toss it.

Air-tight containers for pellets, seed, etc. You may want to freeze or refrigerate these foods, so choose containers of appropriate size, shape and composition for the job.

Cleaning supplies.

• *Dishwashing liquid and diluted bleach* (half a cup of bleach to a gallon of water). Better still, use an "oxygen-activated" cleaner (generally a sodium carbonate/sodium percarbonate formula); it's relatively non-toxic and doesn't rust metal.

• *Assorted plastic-bristled brushes* for cleaning dishes, perches, toys and so on; include a bottle brush if you use a water bottle.

Hand towels. Buy several dozen shop towels at your local home supply store.

• *Paper towels*, rolls and rolls of them.

First-aid kit. See Section 5, Keeping your cockatoo healthy.

41

TAKING YOUR COCKATOO HOME

The first day. Transport your bird in a carrier placed on the floor of the car or strapped to the seat.

It's so big out there!
Photo by Feathered Follies

Make the trip early so she has some time to acclimate before bedtime. A young bird may prefer to spend the first night in her carrier.

Introducing the family.

• *Children.* Make it a family affair with adults in charge. Never, we repeat, leave a child alone with a cockatoo.

• *Cats and dogs.* Most cats (note the qualifier) are okay. Whatever your cockatoo's size her beak is a great deterrent. Not so dogs: a wolf is a wolf is a wolf. What's more, bacteria found on the teeth and claws of dogs and especially cats can be deadly. Marks or no marks, get her to the vet after a close encounter with *any* predatory animal.

42

• *Other birds.* If raised with other birds a cockatoo usually behaves well toward them (see

"I tot I taw a puttytat."
Available at many pet stores is a floor mat that shocks cats and dogs away from your bird's cage.

above regarding companion birds). If raised alone however she may be aggressive. Either way, observe a precautionary six-week quarantine in a separate room (to avoid cross-contamination of toys, bowls, etc.) then move their cages close together for a few weeks before bringing them into contact.

• *Small animals*, including birds, may not survive a cockatoo.

The first six months.

• *Have the bird examined* by a veterinarian qualified in bird care (it is imperative that you verify the veterinarian's avian-care credentials; see Section 6. Keeping your cockatoo healthy). Do so ASAP and definitely within the period specified by contract.

• *Give her plenty of space*, i.e., peace and quiet, to adjust. Set nap-times. Limit visitors.

• *Establish her diet.* (Section 4. Nurturing your cockatoo.)

• *Keep her wings trimmed* (Section 4).

• *Get to know her.* Consult her previous caretaker, do some reading, observe her behavior.

• *Learn to handle her.* Ask your bird shop or avian veterinarian.

• *Practice step-up* in order to pattern cooperation. (Section 6. Training your cockatoo.)

• *Play peekaboo* with a towel to get her used to it. (Section 6.)

• *Teach her to play alone* with a mix of toys, thus encouraging curiosity and learning rather than attention-seeking. *We can't stress enough how important this is.*

• *Don't expect too much too soon.* Cockatoos are long-lived, free-wheeling creatures with no particular sense of urgency. What's more they're confirmed reactionaries, loving routine to a fault and consequently resisting change.

𝕿𝖍𝖔𝖚 𝕾𝖍𝖆𝖑𝖙 𝕹𝖔𝖙:

• Use Teflon cookware anywhere near your bird, especially in an enclosed area; when heated it emits a deadly gas. Ditto the oven-cleaning cycle.

• Feed your bird avocado. *Ever.* Avoid alcohol, caffeine and chocolate as well.

• Salt your bird's food or feed her items such as canned goods, crackers or pretzels (even human presidents have been known to choke on them) that have a high salt content.

• Leave your bird outside her cage unattended.

• Leave your bird in the care of a child.

• Place your bird in a dangerous situation, e.g., near house plants that may be poisonous.

• Covet thy neighbor's really *fabulous* Moluccan.

43

3

Understanding Your Cockatoo

BIRD BRAIN

Have we mentioned that parrots are smart? A recent study puts them right up there with chimps and dolphins. Having followed a different evolutionary path, your cockatoo's brain is built differently than a mammal's--something about clusters instead of layers-- yet is equally complex, adaptable and creative. What's more it comes with a built-in pilot's license. Size? Relatively speaking, even a crow's brain is as large as a chimpanzee's.

Parrots can understand and express number, color, material properties, the difference

A rainbow coalition
Photo by Robert Tudor

45

between absence and presence and many other abstract concepts. African grays in particular are lab certified to converse with people, create syntax and teach other grays what they learn.

The upside of all this is new respect for bird brains. The downside? Birds may soon replace lab rats for investigating functional neuroanatomy.

IN EVERY COCKATOO A GREMLIN LURKS

Remember *Gremlins*, the Spielberg film? Well, your cockatoo is a kinder, gentler version of those movie-mythical creatures. Cute, playful, cuddly. But don't turn your back on her. Her curiosity is boundless, her beak is a weapon of mass destruction, and she's *always* looking for trouble. Worst of all she has an addictive personality. Too much cuddling, for instance, may lead to over-preening followed by feather-picking and other attention-getting behavior such as screaming or banging the bars with her beak like a film noir jailbird with his tin cup.

In every cockatoo a gremlin lurks
Photo by Feathered Follies

IS THAT NORMAL?

What makes a cockatoo tick? Like all sentient beings she behaves according to some combination of nature and nurture. While we're nowhere near breaking the code, one thing is certain: cockatoos are prey animals and act accordingly. When a heavyweight boxer bites an ear he's being aggressive; when a cockatoo bites an ear she's (probably) being defensive.

BEHAVIOR IN THE WILD

Cockatoos join flocks for practical ends: greater efficiency in locating food and sleeping places, mate selection, and, of course, safety in numbers. Flock sizes range from eight to ten members for jungle species and up to thousands for the plains and desert species of Australia. Except

Why the un-caged bird sings
Photo by Andy Cranston

aggression even when their numbers are large and individuals have little personal space. In breeding season, however, mates develop an urge for considerably more such space, ultimately dropping out of the flock to find a nice quiet suburb for mates, who bond for life, there are no strong ties among members. Neither is there any discernible "pecking order": in a large, constantly re-forming flock, the maintenance of a rigid hierarchy would be all-consuming. As a rule, members of the flock eat, sleep and groom together, instantaneously transferring moods and communicating through a variety of signals both aural (contact calls) and visual (body language, mobile crest). Most species have also developed sentinel systems in which a few members stand watch while the rest of the flock feeds.

Group behavior trumps individual behavior, so members rarely exhibit serious

That's close enough!
Photo by Andy Cranston

47

and rear a family. For nests they favor ready-made holes, usually high in the trees, but often in the cavities of fallen tree trunks, rock formations, escarpments and termite mounds. Most jungle species seek out the same nest hole year after year.

Nest Holes

Many wild cockatoos like to nest in the cavities of fallen trees. In rural Australia, however, dead trees are harvested for firewood and on private land have no legal protection as nesting sites (they are protected on some public preserves). The resultant loss of natural nest holes may contribute to the rapid decline of some cockatoo populations, the rare black varieties in particular. Encroaching civilization has also brought about habitat loss and predation by imported animals, such as the ring-tailed opossum.

Home schooling. Like people, birds are born with certain abilities and predispositions, but have to learn most of what they need to know about the world. In the wild a young bird learns the basics from his parents; then, weaned and fledged, follows them into a flock. There he learns to socialize, forage, evade enemies, and so forth, ultimately finding a mate of his own and renewing the cycle. In the severely circumscribed world of your family room, however, *you* have to teach him what

48

he needs to know, about showers and pellets and toys and what to fear and what not, plus the ground rules for sharing a human nest. The first year is crucial: it shapes the rest of his life.

Protecting the flock. Your bird will act instinctively to protect his flock, i.e., you and the other members of his household. If he gets the idea you aren't in control he'll take over and deal with perceived threats such as your big-haired Aunt Doris according to his abilities. The moral: *stay in control.* Don't be intimidated. Keep him off your head and shoulders; use step-up commands; be calm, firm and persistent. Every time you ask him to do something and he complies your flock leadership is reinforced. But don't get cocky: the will to power is not limited to human beings.

Busybodies

Nutritionally specialized animals such as Gang-gang cockatoos minimize the Darwinian competition for food. Wild Gang-gangs spend most of their time shelling the hard millet-sized seeds of peppermint eucalyptus, a food of no interest to most creatures. Thus born to be busy, caged Gang-gangs require activities galore to ward off boredom.

Drop a seed lose a seed
Photo by Robert Tudor

atoo, whose not-so-latent ancestral memories include a wide variety of vicious night prowlers. All the more reason to respect her afternoon naps.

Bedding down for the night can be mildly contentious. Since

BEHAVIOR IN CAPTIVITY

The cockatoo at rest. The healthy cockatoo rests and sleeps on one leg with the other drawn up into her feathers. She may also tuck her head in her back feathers, and close, or partially close, her eyes. But as a prey animal she sleeps lightly. Wouldn't you? Say you learned of a burglar in your neighborhood, wouldn't you snap awake at every sound? So, instinctually, does your recently "civilized" cock-

Keep an eye out, dear
Photo by Andy Cranston

49

your bird likes to be with the flock and considers herself every bit your equal, she may object particularly to sleeping in another room. Says the child: "Just a little while longer, mommy,

The cockatoo at play. Ingenious and fun-loving, cockatoos devise games and toys and cavort about like truant kids, demonstrating a similarly high level of adaptability, memory and propensity for play: what we humans call intelligence. Zygodactyl dexterity also contributes to intelligence; indeed the physical means to implement ideas, to experiment and learn from success and failure are key to intellectual development. Unprompted, cockatoos employ

Toys are me!

pleeeeeease? or else I'll screech
50 my head off for as long as I can stay awake." To which the adult replies: "When dinosaurs fly, young lady. What you need is ten hours' sleep in a cage in a reasonably dark, quiet room." Be gentle but firm. (See also Section 6. Training your cockatoo).

tools much better than chimps. The objects Coco uses to scratch her head? Adaptation. In the wild she'd have a mate to preen her.

Try to be as smart and inventive as your bird about the toys you give her. The

of cloth, clothespins and the like throughout the day. She also unstacks and (occasionally) stacks plastic cups, twists nuts off bolts, picks locks and...but enough said.

In addition to picking the right toys, change them out regularly to prevent boredom and keep the gremlin at bay.

A nip here/A tuck there/ Happy Holidays

best ones have moving parts that turn or twist or unhook or stack or link together. Nearly every morning, Coco attaches a plastic chain to the clapper of a bell hung from the ceiling of her cage, then adds key rings, strips

Not all play, of course, is smart; some is pure tomfoolery. In the wild cockatoos joust each other with their beaks. You'll see the same behavior when your own pride-and-joy attacks a bell or a ball or her own mirror image; the antics can get crazy. Like Amazons, cockatoos are also fond of "catch me if you can," an exciting game that often ends with a yelp and a

51

bloodied human appendage. (Note: the Goffin's especially has a human toe fetish, so watch out.)

As she matures, of course, your playful, inventive cockatoo will become a bit more, well, grown up, but neither less amusing nor less needful of amusement.

Working out. For cockatoos play and exercise are inseparable and together constitute a way of life. They're forever climbing, swinging, scratching, stretching, playing with (or throwing) their toys or their food. Denizens of the plains and deserts are especially good on their feet and often run or hop about the cage. Some like to scratch on the floor or the furniture and particularly the smaller species love to shred newspaper. Not surprisingly they like to fly, as well, as will your bird if given the chance, placing both her and your possessions at risk. Keep her wings clipped and provide opportunities for flapping, as on a gym or a climbing tree. You can also grasp her claws with your thumb as she sits on your hand and gently swing her about. Not only is exercise healthy, it also helps relieve nervous energy that can lead to screaming and feather-picking.

And the beak goes on. In order to clean her beak the

Hangin' out

cockatoo strops it on a hard surface. Supply a mineral or concrete perch for this purpose; it also keeps her beak in shape. Beak grinding is normal comfort behavior, just before a nap, say, or in anticipation of a good night's sleep. Listen to it for long it'll put you to sleep too. Stretching and yawning--gaping with the beak-- after naps are normal as well. Gaping may also relieve an itch, say in her ear or at the corner of her beak, or simply provide passive amusement of the thumb-twiddling variety. Like any other behavior, however, if it seems compulsive-obsessive

52

consult your veterinarian or behaviorist. With regard to chewing, cockatoos are notorious for it. Keep her supplied with things to sink her beak into besides your fingers and heir-looms. (See Section 2: Taking your cockatoo home, for advice on toys.)

Which brings us to "beaking" and biting. A young cockatoo's beaking is like a human toddler's sampling the environment. A lit-tle mud, a grasshopper, an old shoe. Rather than biting she's experiencing the world, so don't over-interpret a soft gnaw on your finger. Biting, on the other hand, is symptomatic of fear or anger or territoriality. Once in a while it happens. Hey, tempers flare. Again, though, if it becomes persistent it's a problem. (See Section 6.)

Vocalization.

• *Bird chat.* Goffin's and Bare-eyed cockatoos are particularly prone to monologues that might be dialogues if only you could respond in kind. When she talks to you like that think of yourself talking to your cat or your spouse or the bathroom mirror.

• *Mimicking.* When it comes to human speech cock-atoos can't compete with Amazons and African Grays, nor are their high-pitched voices as suitable. Yet they

Anthropomorphizing Coco

About birds (and the cosmos generally) Albert Einstein said, "It's all relative." Illustrating this insight, Dr. Theodore Barber, author of The Human Nature of Birds, tells us birds are no more instinctually driven than we are. While both man and bird are programmed to carry out their species' specialties they also learn and adapt, partly because of their ability to exchange information though language.

All right, I'll wear it - but no feather!

"Like non-literate human beings living in the wild they communicate...to their flock mates everything that is relevant or of interest to them [such as] the rain, the animals, food, water, mating, offspring and so on." What's more they intelligently adapt to changes in habitat, food supply, mates and the like; play with a passion similar to that of human children; experience the same fundamental feelings and emotions as humans"; and have a sense of the beauti-ful, a general aesthetic sense just as humans

53

do, for instance composing and singing songs (in duets, trios, quartets and even quintets, antiphonally or polyphonically) that human musicians admire.

For Charlie Parker it was an honor to be nicknamed "Bird."

Even so, most scientists reject anthropomorphism. Birds are simply inferior, they sniff, unworthy of comparison with human beings. Really? Is it objective, much less scientific, to compare "us" (a single species at the top of its class) to "them" (an average of all avian species lumped together and divided by 9,000)? And when scientists compare a parrot's intelligence to that of a young child, they mean human child, right?

Anyway what do such comparisons imply? Clearly not much. What if we woke up tomorrow with wings instead of arms and hands? We'd fly instead of walk, ridding the world simultaneously of automobiles and airplanes; we'd be unable to make or use any but the simplest of tools, forcing us to adapt to the environment rather than alter the environment to suit our whims; and if zygodactyl we'd eat with our feet. What if we woke up with beaks instead of lips? Our language would

simplify and so, as a result, would our ability to think reflectively, as I'm doing now. What if we woke up in trees and foraged for seed and evaded pythons and scratched for grubs and laid eggs and hatched them and migrated around the world, all without succor from the CBS Survivor crew?

So no, birds aren't smart as we are, not on our terms; they can't drive cars or grill steaks or fry potatoes or turn on air conditioners or fire missiles at each other, because, for one thing, they aren't built that way, and, for another, they aren't that stupid.

So yes, when Coco was younger we called her the Duchess of Whinger when we took her out of her sleeping cage and she whinged like a baby for the nipple. We still tell each other how smart she is when she picks a new lock, and grin proudly as parents at a school play when she performs her cockatoo stunts. But at the same time we realize she's a bird and treat her accordingly, giving her space to be all she can be, doing our best to care for this lovable and smart but very different creature we Martians have abducted and caged.

What's that, Coco? No, you can't sleep with us tonight. Well...

can certainly learn human words and phrases. Often the wrong ones. Also the least pleasant body sounds of you and yours, including pets. Contrary to belief, however, parrots don't mimic very much in the wild. Why should they? In the wild they have their own language. So when your bird mimics your words or sounds or the sounds of your pets, please

remember that what she says she's learned from, and for, you. (See Section 6, Training your cockatoo, for tips on expanding her human vocabulary.)

• *Screaming*. Occasionally your cockatoo will emit sounds like the screech of a rusty steam shovel. The bigger the louder; Moluccans have been known to break crystal three miles away (just kidding). This is

"Why can't they speak our language?"
Photo by Everett Butler

compulsive screaming there are steps you can take to ameliorate it. First and foremost, if you coddle your bird every time she yelps she'll yelp to get coddled. Child, dog or bird, the rule is constant: rewarding bad behavior reinforces it. Ignore her screams, letting her know it's a no-win game. (By ignore we mean completely: don't respond at all to sounds you don't like. Do not, repeat DO NOT squirt her with water.) Second, look for other possible causes and correct them: small cage, improper lighting, lack or inappropriateness of toys, inadequate gym time, too much time

likely to occur early in the morning, once in a while during the day (sometimes it just *feels* good to scream) and always in the evening. Grit your teeth and calm your neighbors. It doesn't last long, maybe 15 minutes, and eventually you'll get used to it. If not immune.

• *Compulsive screaming.*
Sometimes the screaming gets entirely out of hand. Bear in mind, however, that your cockatoo is naturally noisy, and that trying to correct innate behavior is psychologically risky. In other words make sure the behavior really *is* abnormal before taking serious action. While there's no sure fix for

I'm all stressed out!"
Photo by Feathered Follies

alone and/or too little human interaction. If the screaming is really bad, try covering her for a few minutes until she quiets down; then remove the cover and give her the attention she wants, thus rewarding her for not screaming. Should the problem persist call your vet or

55

Nervous wreck.

An emotionally sensitive creature, your cockatoo is unduly susceptible to stress. Stress activates the bird's sympathetic nervous system, triggering the release of adrenaline and other hormones that raise her blood pressure, her heart rate and, it follows, her energy level. While a wild bird can vent stress by increasing physical activity, captive birds resort to chewing, climbing or playing--or, if the stress goes unrelieved, to various forms of extreme behavior.

Stress also weakens the immune system, leaving the bird vulnerable to infection by opportunistic organisms. Signs of stress include screaming, biting, fretfulness (hopping or flying perch to perch, constant repetitive movements such as bowing or rocking side to side), apathy, phobic behavior, toe chewing and feather picking. Among the causes of avian stress are:

- Illness
- Allergy or toxic reaction
- Nutritional deficiency or food intolerance
- Loneliness, fear, excess noise

- Breeding season
- Trauma (often as a result of abuse or mishandling)
- Changes in the environment
- Lack of exercise
- Lack of sleep
- Lack of (or change in) routine
- Erratic feeding schedule
- Lack of entertainment
- Lack of interaction with her (human) flock
- Teasing
- Loss of a favorite person or bird
- Introduction off a new pet or family member
- Family problems (yours)

Naturally the best way to treat stress is to find and eliminate the cause. Lack of sleep, for example, triggers all sorts of aberrant behavior. (See above, this section, and Section 4, Nurturing your cockatoo). As a general palliative, try bathing her; beyond its calming effect a warm shower is great "quality time" for you both.

bird behaviorist. (See Section 6, Training your cockatoo.)

Facial expression. Because your cockatoos facial feathers are mobile they provide her with the ability to show her feelings despite that big bony schnoz.

Body language. Hunching the shoulders; flipping, drooping or flapping the wings; wagging, bobbing or fanning the tail; quivering, crouching; holding the body rigid--all

these gestures are part of a cockatoo's repertoire. You'll learn to interpret them through experience and plain old common sense. If she looks and/or acts sick she's probably sick, likewise for angry or hungry. Part of the romance is getting to know her.

Eating habits. A cockatoo shucks the outer skins or hulls of seeds, fruits and vegetables with her beak and tongue. Her claws are used like hands

56

"I'm bad! I'm bad!"
Photo by Everett Butler

to grasp and lift food to the beak. Because food as entertainment is more interesting than food as nourishment more of it winds up on the floor of the cage than in her crop. She may, for instance, play a monotonous game in which she drops a pellet or some other small object on her head, rolls it from shoulder to shoulder, catches it with her wing, picks it out and starts all over again. A boredom exercise, probably, the sort of thing we used to do in middle school. She may also toss food when you put her in her cage ("I'm innocent!") or when you take her out of her cage ("Look what I can do!")

Doing the moves.

Avian body language is hardly a science. What's more it varies from species to species, bird to bird and context to context. That said, some of the more common signals are:

• The rouse. When your cockatoo ruffles and shakes her plumage she's expressing pleasure of a special kind, say when a favorite person enters the room, or she's in a favorite place.

• The tail wag. The wag often accompanies the rouse and means about the same thing (except after a bath, when it's just her way of straightening the feathers being wagged).

• The tail fan. In most birds fanning is associated with courtship: a Keep Off sign for intruders. In cockatoos, however, it may simply express apprehension, as when meeting a new person.

• The crouch. Leaning forward, your cockatoo holds her folded wings slightly away from her body. This is get-ready-get-set-to-fly mode. Maybe she wants to go somewhere but isn't sure where; or maybe she's saying, "Let me out of this bloody cage!"

• The preen. Preening in your presence means she's comfortable with you. Chest and tail preening particularly imply a strong sense of trust and security.

• The wing stretch. Stretching her wings over her legs relaxes the bird's flight muscles, and, like preening, is generally practiced when she's completely at ease.

• The beak grind. Grinding together the upper and lower mandibles helps maintain the beak. It also signifies contentment, as when the flock is together and evening grows nigh.

• The face fluff. Typically, a fluffy face is a happy face.

"Diet? I've tried them all"
Photo by Dey Alexander

or at any time of day while she's in her cage ("What am I, a potted plant?").

Preening. The cockatoo preens feather by feather, working toward the tail, several times a day; then with head and beak powders and scours her entire plumage. She may also scratch her head a lot, even using a stick or toy to help (a use of tools that would make a chimp proud). Slow, deliberate head scratching is common among single birds, probably to satisfy a need for allopreening (mutual preening among mates and other members of the same species, known as "conspecifics").

Touching up
Photo by Feathered Follies

Allopreening not only keeps inaccessible feathers healthy but also contributes to emotional bonding. Hence scratching the bird's head and other unreachables should be a frequent and consistent part of your relationship with her.

Hissing. Stay clear.

Sneezing. Unless it's persistent don't worry; things get up cockatoo nostrils, too, including their own claws (yes, they do pick their noses).

Pinning or flashing. Parrots' irises contract and expand quickly when they're angry or excited. This is called "pinning." Cockatoos however have eyes so dark they're all but impossible to read.

FEAR OF CHANGE

For all her curiosity, adventurousness and creativity, your cockatoo is a creature of habit. The familiar is safe, the unfamiliar is not. So if yesterday your hair was red and today it's blonde, or you had a beard and now you don't, or you walk in with something strange in your hand or on your head (for some reason baseball caps are especially terrifying), your drama queen may react adversely and altogether out of proportion. Same goes for surprises: no quick moves or sudden appearances around the corner.

59

SEX AND THE SINGLE COCKATOO

In the wild, mating behavior is stimulated by light, humidity, temperature, food supply, non-verbal communication with conspecifics, etc., and heightens as the days grow longer. In a cage in a house in a city, however, the artificial environment confuses things: like winter in Montana, breeding season may come any time before or after Fourth of July.

During this period your cockatoo may be aroused (although many couldn't care less) by anything resembling a nesting cavity--a box, a cabinet, that space in the bookshelf where your Webster's used to go--and especially by physical stimulation. Avoid petting under his wings, pulling his tail, grasping his body, wrestling with his beak or touching his back or rump. A la Portnoy, he may rub his vent against your hand or leg--or, frankly, anything--for gratification.

Aggressive behavior such as biting is common in these trying times, so be sure he's stick-trained (see Section 5, Training your cockatoo) and in all events *keep him off your shoulder.* Perching next to your face (the "talking head") is like sharing a branch. He may get defensive of your shoulder as his nesting territory and you as his mate and...let's just say the situation can get out of hand. Typically, though, all you have to do when he acts up is to put him

in his cage or on his T-stand and ignore him. Sex, of course, is always a complex issue, but much of what's going on is displacement behavior. Don't take it personally. Remember when your hormones raged? (Which isn't to say they're not raging right now.)

THE BIRD BEHAVIORIST

Should your bird consistently bite, scream, pick her feathers or act otherwise neurotic, and no effort on your part cures her (see Section 5, Keeping your cockatoo healthy, and Section 6, Training your cockatoo), contact a bird behaviorist.

The school of human psychology called "behaviorism" focuses strictly on observable behavior, altogether disregarding emotion and motive. Bird behaviorists, on the contrary, take a broader view. As results-oriented psychological therapists they're aware of your cockatoo's intelligence and complex emotional makeup. Indeed most of them would agree that her emotional response to past environmental stimuli--say, being caged in the basement for months--is probably the source of her present conduct. But with no common language the behaviorist can't subject your bird to analysis, Freudian or otherwise. Ultimately, all he has to go on is his knowledge of birds, his skills of observation and his experience in similar cases.

Some behaviorists are veterinarians; others have specialized degrees in, say, animal behavior; still others got their know-how from years of dealing first-hand with birds. Just make sure yours comes recommended. They don't come cheap and you don't want bad advice.

Figure an hour for the initial interview, usually by phone. You may have to fill out a questionnaire. Don't hold back; if for any reason there's a lot of stress around your home let the behaviorist know. Don't be embarrassed about your ignorance; that's what experts are for. Don't talk, listen; you're paying for the expert's advice. And don't argue for the sake of it; you'll only frustrate the behaviorist and further inflate a fee already balooning from billable chit-chat.

Palm Cockatoo
Photo by Everett Butler

61

4

Nurturing Your Cockatoo

"Feed me!"
Photo by Ginger Russell

THE COCKATOO EFFECT

You've heard of the "butterfly effect?" It's an axiom of chaos theory which says,

roughly, that under certain "initial conditions" a flutter of wings in Maui can blow up a storm in Hong Kong. There's also a "cockatoo effect." Either you keep up with the bird chores, or your house, and consequently your life, will become a shambles. The principal victim though will be the bird herself, whose life depends literally on you.

Hygiene. A mess of cockatoos, continued. They produce oodles of powder, and during warm weather replace their feathers almost continually. So there's considerable sweeping and dusting to be done. Also, as already mentioned, they're terrible slobs. Keep her cage and utensils clean; the fungus and bacteria that proliferate in filth are dangerous. What's more her accumulated feather dust can affect not only her respiratory health but also yours and that of your family.

On a daily basis:

• Change the cage liner (preferably newspaper).

• Clean dishes and bottles. If using a water bottle, test the nozzle to assure it works; birds dehydrate fast.

• Use a hand vacuum and water/soap mixture in a spray bottle to clean cage, perches and surroundings.

Every day or so:

• Rotate toys; the boredom factor can't be overstressed.

As needed:

• Remove and clean soiled perches, toys, etc. Wood, rope and plastic can go in the dishwasher.

Every few weeks:

• Scrub cage, gym, perches, trays, etc., then sterilize with either an oxygen-activated cleaner or a solution of 1/2 cup bleach to one gallon water. For big jobs try a self-service car wash.

"Towel, please"

Grooming

Baths and showers.

Some birds like water more than others. A jungle bird, especially, will need help to

64

keep her skin moist and her powder under control. If you shower with your bird be careful taking her from a hot, steamy bathroom to some cooler area of the house. Give her time to dry naturally or use a hair dryer on low heat held well away from the feathers. Most cockatoos love showers--spreading their wings and fanning their tails and flapping and getting soaked--as well as the pampering that goes with it.

Keep in mind, however, that taking a shower is learned behavior. A novice bird should be introduced to it gradually. Start by misting her regularly with a spray bottle that has never contained dangerous chemicals. (For really touchy 'toos there are near-silent misters on the market.) Once inured, she's ready for a weekly soaking. Hold her far enough back from the shower that the water won't frighten or overwhelm her and avoid spraying into her eyes. Also keep her from drinking too much water. If the bird reacts badly to human-style bathing don't traumatize her by forcing the issue. Eventually, though, she should learn to take a proper bath, so if at first you don't succeed.

If you have an itchy cockatoo it's probably dry skin. This is a problem in climates requiring constant air conditioning or heating. In such cases we strongly recommend a humidifier: not a dinky steam vaporizer, but a cool air, heavy-duty humidifier. (More *stuff*? Sorry. Remember you're simulating nature.) Keep the humidity around the cage at 60 percent or so.

Shampoo the bird no more than once a month so as to maintain her natural feather oils. Use shampoos formulated for cockatoos, available either from your retailer or online.

Parasites. Provided your bird comes from a reputable source and has not been raised outdoors with access to the ground, she's not likely to have parasites, either internal or external. If you suspect them nonetheless consult your veterinarian.

CAUTION: avoid over-the-counter remedies. Too often unregulated, they may do more harm than the pests they kill.

Trims and Pedicures. If at all possible leave the trimming of nails and wings to a professional; that way you know it's done right and your bird hates somebody else instead of you. Check the groomer's credentials and get recommendations.

No professional groomer in your vicinity?

Then buy a good pair of scissors and a nail file and proceed as follows:

65

Claws. Blunt the bird's claws when they get so sharp they hurt you. Wrap her in a towel, firmly grasp one claw at a time and blunt it with a nail file. GO EASY: blunt her claws too much she can't feed herself properly or even grip her perch, let alone do all that climbing she loves.

Wings. Your bird must learn how

File claws just enough to blunt them
Photo by Ginger Russell

to fly; failure to do so may produce both psychological and physical damage. On the other hand you can't permit her to soar about freely. First, she may escape; second, she may injure herself (beware ceiling fans!); third, she may become so independent that she rejects your authority. Rule of thumb: when she starts to fly straight (on a level) or upward (achieving lift) it's time to trim her flight feathers.

Let's start with some definitions: The first ten longest feathers of the wing are the *primary flight feathers* ("primaries"); the short feathers overlapping these are the *primary coverts* ("coverts"). *Blood* or *pin* feathers are unopened, new-growth feathers covered by a waxy membrane and amply supplied with blood. *Avoid blood feathers absolutely.*

Once she fledges, trim the first four primaries; this allows her to fly but not too high. Add the fifth primary in the second clip, and perhaps the sixth or seventh, depending on the bird, in subsequent clips. *Never clip at or above the coverts.* A bad clip may cause your bird to fall repeatedly, producing injuries and undermining self-confidence. Worse still, it may lead to feather chewing or picking; difficult to break, such habits may permanently damage your bird's plumage.

Here's how to clip her wings the right way:

a) If necessary, restrain her in a towel.

b) Carefully spread out the wing and examine for blood (pin) feathers.

c) Trim the outer four to seven primaries about half-way up to the overlying coverts in a shape approximating the curve

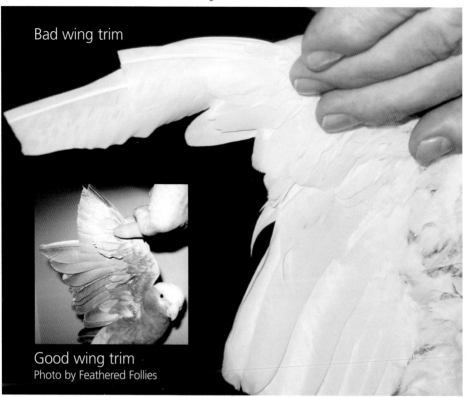

Bad wing trim

Good wing trim
Photo by Feathered Follies

of the coverts.

d) No matter what you've read or been told *do not* leave the first two or three feathers long; among other things, they can get caught and broken, which in turn may lead to, yes, feather chewing et cetera.

e) If you're having a groomer or vet do it, don't trust him unless you know him from experience. When it comes to birds, outdated training and/or poor judgment are all too common. Oversee the procedure and be prepared to intercede.

Beak. Generally a mineral perch will keep her beak honed. Excessive beak growth could mean trouble and calls for professional attention (see Section 5, Keeping your cockatoo healthy).

Feeding. As both an omnivore (with a strong vegetarian tilt) and a forager (she likes her food off the floor as well as out of the bowl) your cockatoo enjoys a wide variety of tastes and textures. Indeed, provided in healthy, tasty combos, variety is the spice of her life. Yet she's also the fussiest of parrots and cautious about

67

accepting food. In a word, fickle. Don't give in to her whims. Go on serving the proper foods until she learns to eat them. Or at least some of them.

Some of the bird food display at Feathered Follies, Lafayette, California

Pelletized formulas provide the best balance of nutrients, including vitamins and minerals, so they should compose about 70 percent of her diet. Keep them available at all times.

Fruits and vegetables. Your cockatoo also needs fresh foods. Try cutting them in small pieces so she won't just sample and toss the big chunks. Corn on the cob, almost anything in the pod-- peas, snow peas, green beans, wax beans--and hot peppers, preferably jalapenos with lots of seeds, the hotter the better. Also broccoli, cauliflower, carrots and carrot tops, cucumbers, spinach, celery, cooked potatoes, sweet potatoes, yams, pumpkin and squash. Ah, yes, and the occasional mixed salad of endive, celery, radicchio and such.

Keep in mind that she too has likes and dislikes. Experiment.

Cockatoos aren't great fruit eaters but they will partake. Pomegranates are good, and itsy-bitsy champagne grapes. So are pears, plums, peaches, raisins, cherries, bananas, mangos, papayas, kiwis, sundry berries, red currants and apples.

CAUTION: apple, pear and peach pits may be poisonous (pardon the alliteration).

Always wash fresh foods thoroughly.

In winter, serve your bird sprouted feeds like oats and wheat. Unseasoned frozen veggies are fine, too; your local grocer stocks a variety of interesting mixtures.

Seeds. Seeds should be included in her diet only as treats and/or as an additive to pellets. Sunflower seed is fatty so limit quantity; likewise pumpkin seeds, nuts, almonds, pine nuts, etc. Don't use moist seeds and generally speaking don't add new seed to old; either can go bad and spoil the barrel.

Protein. Complete, i.e., animal protein is important. No Aussie grubs? No worries. Most pellets include plenty of protein to take their place. You can also treat your bird to boiled egg, tuna or baby food (turkey-and-veggies, say, mixed with pablum and strained fruit). By the way, cockatoo eating chicken is no more cannibalistic than man eating cow.

Human food. Toasted oat and corn bran cereals are good, as well as whole grain bread and dried bananas (watch for preservatives). Again, variety is the spice of a cockie's life. But you are in control. Use your imagination and watch what your bird eats so you can choose accordingly.

Although she can share your food, don't give her too much: all that salt and seasoning. As for junk food--french fries, tortilla chips--cockatoos like it just as much as people do and it's as just bad for them as it is for us. CAUTION: avocado will kill her. Also avoid caffeine, chocolate, alcohol, and

spoiled food (if in doubt throw it out).

Never ever let her eat from your mouth. Human saliva is swimming with bad little bugs.

Water. Provide fresh water daily, more often in warm climates. If

Table 1 - Foods to avoid
Alcohol
Avocado
Caffeine
Candy and other sugary foods
Chocolate
Eggplant
Fatty foods
Fried foods
Milk and milk products
Pickles, chips, hot dogs and other salty foods
Processed foods with high preservative content
Raw mushrooms
Raw or undercooked meats of any kind
Rhubarb
Spoiled foods

your tap water is of low quality use filtered water. Always use a clean bowl.

General. In the mornings when she's hungriest feed her strictly pellets, veggies and fruits. Also great for breakfast are formulated mixes packed with healthy legumes and such;

Table 2
Within a day of hatching a cockatoo can hear you perfectly; between two and two-and-a-half weeks of age, depending on species, her eyes are fully open; and within five months she's fully feathered and ready to face the world.

WEIGHT RANGE OF CHICKS
(In Grams)

AGE	CUMB	CTRI	CROS	CCIT	CLES	CMOL	CBAR	CGAL	CGOF
Hatch	11-21	11-19	7-12	12-15	8-15	16-22	8-14	18	9
1 wk	25-48	24-52	15-27	26-37	20-39	33-48	18-33	46	25
2 wks	72-133	78-134	35-77	78-101	58-105	89-123	48-103	129	79
3 wks	160-253	171-23	167-146	148-197	122-203	171-261	99-186	235	144
4 wks	263-400	268-362	114-181	208-305	213-282	320-433	167-265	385	218
6 wks	436-606	407-542	205-301	319-431	313-380	608-706	283-364	658	300
7 wks	486-646	433-569	240-305	320-448	314-404	686-790	289-385	729	304
8 wks	497-663	416-600	225-292	319-437	325-390	738-855	302-375	750	289
9 wks	492-679	406-576	220-289	296-428	308-373	759-885	238-346	757	271
12 wks	440-591	356-495	237-309	308-367	229-358	734-900	268-314	677	265
14 wks	404-589	365-482	248-299	282-390	236-366	686-826	280-336	673	260

(Highlighted areas indicate maximum weights)
KEY TO ABREVIATIONS

CUMB Umbrella cockatoo
CTRI Triton cockatoo
CROS Rose-breasted cockatoo
CCIT Citron cockatoo
CLES Lesser sulfur-crested cockatoo

CMOL Moluccan cockatoo
CBAR Bare-eyed cockatoo
CGAL Greater sulfur-crested cockatoo
CGOF Goffin's cockatoo

once cooked, they can be frozen in ice cube containers and thawed in the microwave. Seeds, nuts and treats, in modest portions, can help relieve her afternoon boredom. Grit? For chickens, maybe, for cockatoos, no.

Body weight. Very young and old birds may need more feed to maintain body weight, but don't overdo it; obesity is as bad for your bird as it is for you and will almost certainly cut her life short. Weight loss despite eating well may indicate illness.

The sleeping cage. Some cockatoos will sleep contentedly in their cages with little ado, while others, for their reasons or yours, will be better off in a sleeping cage. Some will sleep without being covered, while others, again for their reasons or your own, will require a cage cover (be sure it shuts out the light with-

Table 3
AVERAGE ADULT WEIGHT
(In Grams)

	CUMB	CTRI	CROS	CCIT	CLES	CMOL	CBAR	CGAL	CGOF
Male	583	582	338	412	366	874	358	849	306
Female	526	524	307	341	307	794	337	789	246

KEY TO ABREVIATIONS

CUMB	Umbrella cockatoo	CMOL	Moluccan cockatoo
CTRI	Triton cockatoo	CBAR	Bare-eyed cockatoo
CROS	Rose-breasted cockatoo	CGAL	Greater sulfur-crested cockatoo
CCIT	Citron cockatoo	CGOF	Goffin's cockatoo
CLES	Lesser sulfur-crested cockatoo		

Table 4
APPROXIMATE AGE OF FULL PLUMAGE

	CUMB	CTRI	CROS	CCIT	CLES	CMOL	CBAR	CGAL	CGOF
In Weeks	16	19	13	12	13	20	16	15	10

KEY TO ABREVIATIONS

CUMB	Umbrella cockatoo	CMOL	Moluccan cockatoo
CTRI	Triton cockatoo	CBAR	Bare-eyed cockatoo
CROS	Rose-breasted cockatoo	CGAL	Greater sulfur-crested cockatoo
CCIT	Citron cockatoo	CGOF	Goffin's cockatoo
CLES	Lesser sulfur-crested cockatoo		

out cutting off the air). Through trial and error you'll find a way for you both to get some shut-eye.

LEAVING YOUR BIRD AT HOME

The working household. You work, your spouse works, your kids go to school and your mother-in-law won't birdsit, so for most of the day your cockatoo is home alone.

First of all, make sure the cage is padlocked; if there's a way out your 'too will find it. Second, leave her plenty of water, food (seed and pellets; serve the fresh stuff only when you're there to assure against spoilage) and a variety of toys, chewables and things to shred. Third, leave the radio on a continuous music station: silence is not for cockatoos. Finally, if you're getting back after dark, leave a light on. Better yet, buy a lamp or two with timers or light sensors. Like all kids cockatoos are scared of things that go bump in the night. Leaving her alone overnight is inadvisable but sometimes unavoidable.

Fighting without fighting
Illustrated by
Natalie Love Adams Atalina's Creations

Kung Fu.

In the cult movie "Enter the Dragon," Bruce Lee describes his martial arts style as "the art of fighting without fighting," which he proceeds to demonstrate by setting his would-be opponent adrift in a boat.

So try a little Kung Fu on your irascible bird. If her body language says "Don't touch," hey, don't touch. Instead figure out what's wrong...

- Is she excited or frightened?
- Did something startle her?
- Does she have some physical need?
- Is she hurt or ill?
- Is she protesting your attention to something else?
- Did you point your finger at her?
- Did you invade her space (e.g., cage)?

...then eliminate the effect by eliminating the cause.

Longer is unconscionable.

Pet sitters and boarding facilities. If you're going on a trip and simply can't take your bird along, you can either hire a pet sitter, trade pet sitting with another bird owner of your acquaintance and trust, or take the bird to a boarding facility.

Pet sitters. If you hire a sitter she should a) specialize in birds; b) come highly recommended by your veterinarian or bird shop and by two or more clients; c) be bonded; and d) get along with your bird. Clarify terms: how often will she visit, what will she do and what will she charge. Leave her your contact information--hotel, travel agent, whatever--as well as the numbers of a local friend or relative and your vet and emergency care facility. (See Section 7, Forms, checklists and records.) Conversely, be sure to take her phone number along so you can check in once in a while. Take every precaution; failure to do so may have dire consequences.

Apart from caring for your bird and other pets, sitters will often bring in your mail, water your plants and so forth. The good ones are worth their weight in gold. Even the best, however, will be checking on your cockatoo only once or twice a day; anything that happens in between, such as escape or injury, will go unnoticed until her next appointed round.

Boarding facilities. Generally birds are happier at home and don't like the company of strangers, avian or human. What's more there's danger of disease. But if you know the provider, say, your vet or the shop where you acquired the bird, or if the provider comes recommended by someone you trust, you might want to go this route. Publications such as Bird Talk also recommend boarding facilities (see Further Reading).

In any case give the place a thorough site inspection and make sure it enforces strict health requirements for boarders.

Returning home. When you get back home from a long trip everybody's a little wound up, including your cockatoo, who is acutely aware that you abandoned her. What's more she's developed a new routine while you were gone, and perhaps preferences for other people, so while she remembers you and is overjoyed to see you she may, for that fleeting moment of reencounter, have it in for you. How dare you pop up like this and expect to make up! Stick your finger at me, will you? A soap opera moment. (Again, pardon the anthropomorphism.) Or

maybe she's just overexcited and, again, reacting out of proportion. Either way take it easy. Move slowly, speak softly, offer her a treat and a cuddle. Then ease her into her old routine ASAP.

Bare-eyed Cockatoo
Photo by Feathered Follies

73

5

Keeping Your Cockatoo Healthy

"And a one, and a two,
and a three"
*Reprinted by permission
The Oasis Sanctuary
www.the-oasis.org*

GROWING UP: INFANCY THROUGH ADOLESCENCE

A cockatoo comes out of his egg and into the world naked, blind and helpless, opening his eyes and developing a coat of protec-

But appearances deceive: adulthood comes with experience. As his senses develop he begins to learn about the world around him and with growing strength and curiosity proceeds to explore it, pecking and "beaking" everything in reach. Increasingly active, he starts testing his wings a few months later, making short, awkward flights that end in rough landings. These early solos, called "fledging," are essential to

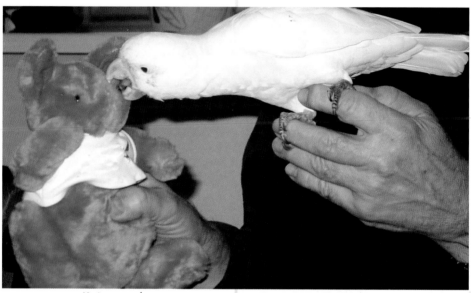

Nosing around

tive down only after several weeks. He'll grow overnight, literally, because in nature he becomes prey for the toothy set, humans included, the instant his egg is laid. Flash forward several months he'll look like a full-grown bird.

both the weaning process and the bird's mental health.

75

He's ready at last for his first cage, where he'll learn to eat solids and drink water (until now supplied through formula) until he can feed himself entirely on his own. With cockatoos this can take a while. Highly sensitive and insecure, they're among the most difficult parrots to wean, the Indonesian species especially. In the wild, 'toos have been observed feeding year-old adolescents. ("Hey, kid, ain't it time you left home?") Be sure yours isn't force-weaned; cockatoos weaned before they're ready are prime candidates for serious behavioral problems.

The fledgling. A growing cockatoo eats a lot and tosses out more. Make pellets available at all times but supplement them heavily with soft foods for a transition period of several months. Buy an electric scale and weigh him at the same time of day once a week, recording the results. Quick weight loss is often the first sign of illness. He needs lots of rest as well, not only 10-12 hours of sleep per night but also a rest period and naps during the day, so keep him out of his cage for limited periods and don't schedule play time during rest time. Bear in mind also that young birds eat all day long; he may become hungry and nervous after an hour or so away from his food.

From weaning to adolescence

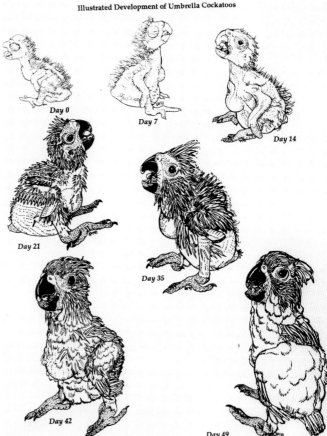

Illustrated Development of Umbrella Cockatoos

Day 0

Day 7

Day 14

Day 21

Day 35

Day 42

Day 49

Fig.1 Stages of development of an Umbrella cockatoo
Illustrations provided by Karen McGovern, Rare Species Conservatory Foundation. Reprinted by permission

is the best of times. A well-reared cockatoo will trust and cooperate with you endlessly. But to everything a season: as in all animals, resistance to authority grows with the onset of sexual maturity. (See Section 3: Understanding your cockatoo).

THE BODY BEAUTIFUL

Your cockatoo is built for lightness and efficiency in the air, yet tough enough to endure Darwinian struggle on the ground. For one thing her bones are hollow. For another her feathers are engineered for protection and flight. Next to her skin, down feathers keep her warm. Covering these and the rest of her body, contour feathers break the wind and rain. Finally, the largest, flight feathers take her airborne. At the base of her tail the preen gland excretes a clear odorless

Fig. 2
Skeletal anatomy of a cockatoo *Illustrated by Natalie Love Adams Atalina's Creations*

oil to waterproof and condition these aerodynamic marvels.

Even the digestive tract is designed for flight, eliminating waste fast and efficiently so as to reduce, as human pilots say, the load factor. Food moves down the esophagus to the crop, where it's stored as it begins the digestive process; then to the stomach; then to

77

the gizzard, which does the job of teeth; then to the intestines and thence to the vent, where solid and fluid wastes are discharged together as droppings.

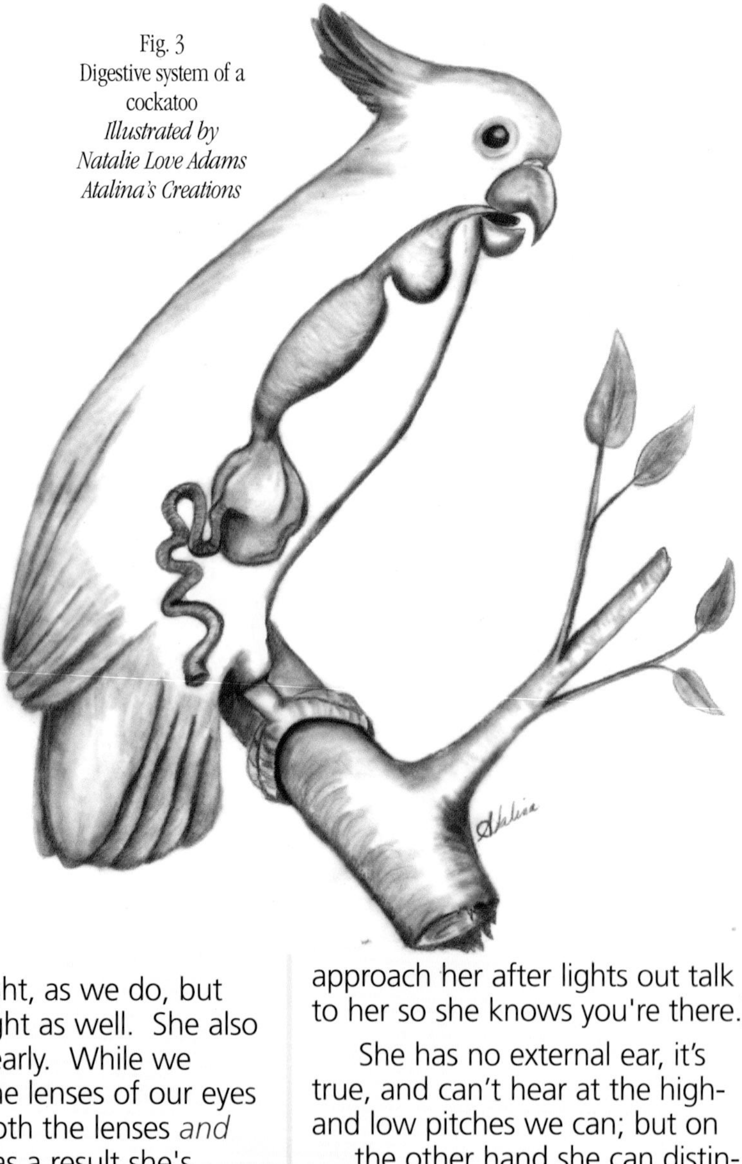

Fig. 3
Digestive system of a
cockatoo
Illustrated by
Natalie Love Adams
Atalina's Creations

Her eyes and rotating head give her a 360-degree field of vision. She can see well both close up and long distance and, yes, in color. Indeed, she sees not only visible light, as we do, but ultra-violet light as well. She also sees more clearly. While we adjust only the lenses of our eyes she adjusts both the lenses *and* the corneas; as a result she's highly sensitive to changes in appearance, sudden moves, and colors. (What she can't do is see in the dark, so if you approach her after lights out talk to her so she knows you're there.)

She has no external ear, it's true, and can't hear at the high- and low pitches we can; but on the other hand she can distinguish more detail in her range of hearing than any among us but the long-term blind. She can also hear the clink of a

78

dish or a sneeze from inside a covered cage behind closed doors located upstairs on the other side of the house.

Her beak (an extension of her skull) is another tough, efficient tool, yet paradoxically quite sensitive; rub it between your thumb and finger and see how she responds. At the exploratory tip of her dry, strong, worm-like tongue are the taste buds. If endowed with fewer of these than you and I (300-400 vs. 9,000) she has roughly the same sensitivity as human beings to salty, sweet, acid and bitter substances. Her sense of smell is comparatively weak, but she can detect the essentials, such as smoke, with great efficiency.

Sight, hearing, smell, taste. What else? Ah, touch. In addition to feeling with her beak, her tongue and her feet, she has tactile nerve endings on her back that sense vibrations, touch, chemicals, heat and changes in air pressure, helping her sense danger from above day or night. Hence her fear of the approaching towel.

Like all parrots (and woodpeckers) the cockatoo has zygodactyl feet--that is, four-toed, with one and four pointing backward and two and three pointing forward--which allow her to climb and grasp as

though with hands. Her claws are designed strictly for gripping, not for use as weapons. She can perch all night on one leg because of an automatic locking mechanism. In cold weather she restricts blood flow to her legs to stay warm, and in warm weather vice-versa.

In the caged bird's debit column is her marvelously efficient respiratory system. Designed for fresh air, it's highly susceptible to all the toxic fumes and pollutants we 'civilized' beings spew into the air. The canary in the coal mine, ring a bell?

CHOOSING A VETERINARIAN

It's scary how incompetent many veterinarians are when it comes to birds. Take care to find someone with specialized training and extensive experience. If at all possible, he should be board certified in avian practice by the American Board of Veterinary Practitioners, in which case the letters DVM (Doctor of Veterinary Medicine) at the end of his name will be followed by ABVP (Avian Practice). At the very least he should belong to the Association of Avian Veterinarians (AAV). Regarding experience, hunt down all the references you can; one or two just won't tell the tale. Consult retailers, breeders *and* the local bird association. You may also contact The Association of Avian Veterinarians (www.aav.org) and the Veterinary Information Network (www.vetquest.com). Finally there are questions of rapport and instinct. Watch the veterinarian handle your bird. Does he act confidently? Does he consider the bird's comfort? Drill him as you would your own brain surgeon and don't be shy about accompanying your bird when samples are taken. To repeat, a cockatoo is not a dog or a cat, not by a long shot, and not simply in the physiological sense. She's downright devious at concealing illness, for instance, which means her veterinarian must see past the facade. Avian specialization and experience are not optional.

SIGNS OF ILLNESS

Since predators are alert to signs of weakness, birds tend to mask illness until they're very sick. If your cockatoo shows symptoms (obvious changes in appearance, posture, condition, behavior or droppings) place her immediately in a warm area (85-90 degrees F) and get her ASAP to the vet. Warmth is crucial. Use an electric blanket or heating pad, assuring cables and controls are well wrapped and hidden. A heat lamp is okay,

too, but less so, because a sick bird needs her sleep.

On the other hand cockatoos come with a long list of caveats. They crave attention, for one thing, and for another they're drama queens. In other words, if your Umbie is upset or has a sore toenail she may do just the opposite of what we've described, pretending to be ill instead of pretending to be well. You can't take chances, of course, but unless the symptoms are severe don't be too annoyed if it's a false alarm.

Diarrhea. Normal droppings consist of feces (green or brown solids), urine (clear liquid) and urates (white solids). Usually your bird defecates and urinates simultaneously, and feeding her foods, such as vegetables, that contain a lot of water increases urine content. So be sure

"I'm a feather picker" - "I'm growing my feathers back"
Photos by Feathered Follies

- •Needle nose pliers, tweezers and scissors
- •Hydrogen peroxide
- •Heating pad
- •An eye dropper and a syringe with the needle removed
- •Energy boosters. A ready-to-mix glucose solution is good. Check with your vet.

it's really diarrhea before getting concerned. Similarly, don't over-react to the presence of other colors (e.g., red or orange); they may simply indicate what she's just eaten (e.g., berries or yam).

FIRST AID: BE PREPARED

Keep handy the names, addresses and telephone numbers of both your veterinarian and an avian after-hours emergency facility (see Section 7, Forms, check-lists and records).

Store first-aid supplies in one place for quick, easy access:

- • Basic bandages, sterile gauze, cotton balls and swabs
- • A towel or two
- • Coagulant - cornstarch and styptic powder
- • Disinfectant - Betadine (provodone iodine solution)

EMERGENCIES

Bleeding. If it's a claw cut too close to the quick use cornstarch or styptic powder. If it's a blood feather, quiet the bird and allow time for the blood to clot on its own. This failing (and provided you're competent at this sort of thing) grip the bleeding feather at its base with a needle-nose pliers and yank it out, then rinse the wound with peroxide and apply pressure until the bleeding stops. **CAUTION**: a wing feather requires support for the hollow, fragile bone above it.

Severe bleeding is an **EMERGENCY**. Apply direct pressure with a finger or a damp towel and get thee to a vet. Do your best to calm the bird; when she's nervous her heart pumps even more blood.

81

Laurie Baker and Stuart Borden

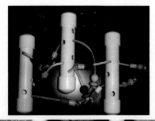

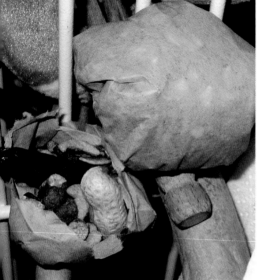

"There's a nut here somewhere." An elaborate
replacement strategy toy from Feather Fu, Austin TX -
Photo by Elizabeth Cantu side-by-side with Photo 60.1
A homemade foraging device. Wrap food in
unbleached coffee bags and attach with wooden
clothespins to bars of cage
Photo by Ginger Russell

82

Also note that moving her from a
cool place to a warm place may
raise her blood pressure and
restart the bleeding.

Bite or scratch wounds from
other animals, especially cats.
EMERGENCY. No visible
injury? Consider shock, inter-

Feather Picking

Your bird will preen off and on throughout the
day, especially at eventide, and more often during molt, which occurs twice yearly and lasts
about three months. You can tell the preening
has become obsessive when she's at it constantly
and between sessions chews on her own shedded
feathers. (While playing with loose feathers is
usually nothing to worry about, do your best to
discourage it; one bad habit leading to another,
who knows?) If preening should graduate to
feather-picking, act fast. You may hear an ouch!
and notice a shiver. The sharp pain, probably
like a needle prick, has triggered an endorphin
"hit." It's theorized that birds become addicted
to endorphins and continue to pluck their feathers for this reason alone. Indeed, once bald spots
appear the behavior is very hard to bring under
control. Homespun remedies abound, and who
knows? some of them may help. Most, though,
don't.

Practically speaking, about all you can do
is identify the cause(s), do your best to remedy it
(them) and then babysit her--give her new and
better things to chew on and keep her otherwise
occupied--while gradually training her out of it.
If however the endorphin theory is correct be
prepared for relapses. CAUTION: The wrong veterinarian (see above) may recommend Valium
or Prozac or what have you for life. Don't you
buy it. There's no proof that such drugs work;
and even if they do, why substitute one addiction
for another? What about her quality of life?
What about the indeterminate consequences to
her mental and physical health? And you, what
about you, how would you even deal with a permanently stoned cockatoo? There are homeo-
pathic remedies on the market as well, but
take care. Like human diet pills, some may
help, some may not, and either way the side
effects could be worse than the ailment.

Typically, feather-picking is triggered by one or more of the following causes:

- Lack of exercise (small cage, no gym, etc.)
- Boredom (lack of toys, interactivity with you, etc.)
- Stress from overcrowded or cramped conditions
- Lack of sleep
- Depression (loss of a mate or close person, etc.)
- Lack of a mate at the onset of sexual maturity
- Skin ailments
- Inappropriate diet
- Low humidity or lack of bathing
- Attention seeking. If you panic every time she picks her feathers she may pick her feathers just to panic you.
- Bad wing trim. (See Section 4. Nurturing your cockatoo.)
- The wing game. She hides a pellet or a seed or a bit of paper beneath her wing, then digs it out, rolls it over her shoulder and hides it under the other wing, and so forth, a tedious game some cockatoos obsess on. Sooner or later a feather gets plucked and becomes the ball in play and then she loses it and plucks another and starts liking the endorphin effect.

Replacement strategies. To avert feather picking or other obsessive behavior, provide your cockatoo with foraging challenges of the sort she'd face in the wild. Zoo veterinarians hide food and create labor-intensive puzzles, "For Satan finds some mischief still/For idle [beaks] to do."

nal bleeding and infection.

Crouching on the perch or sitting on the bottom of the cage with eyes shut and feathers ruffled. Call your vet right away.

Respiratory problems. EMERGENCY. That highly efficient respiratory system is her Achilles heel. Signs of trouble include labored breathing, tail-bobbing and nasal discharge, and by the time you notice it may be too late.

Head injuries. She bangs into a window and knocks herself out. EMERGENCY.

Alimentary problems. Birds can deteriorate rapidly, so if your cockatoo isn't eating or drinking consult the vet right away.

Regurgitation. If accompanied by other signs of illness, see your vet. If not, and the season is spring, it's likely an aspect of courting or nesting behavior. Remain vigilant.

Poisoning. If she can get into it she will. Possible signs: vomiting, diarrhea, convulsions, blood in the droppings, a rash around the beak area. EMERGENCY.

83

Foreign objects. Usually down the gullet, sometimes down the windpipe. EMERGENCY.

Potty problems. Frequent straining or vent protrusions. When you see something protruding from the vent don't yank first and call later; consult your vet immediately.

Heatstroke. Her wings droop, she's listless and panting, she's unsteady on her feet. Move her to a cooler spot and mist her with cool, not cold, water. Make sure she has fresh drinking water. Call your vet if you deem it necessary.

Convulsions or seizures. **EMERGENCY.** Do not stop go go go to the veterinarian.

Burns. **EMERGENCY**. For *boiling water* use cool water. For *grease* use cornstarch. For *acid* use cool water to dilute, then baking soda-and-water paste to neutralize. For *alkali* dilute with cool water and neutralize with vinegar. Call your vet for further instructions.

Broken bones. **EMERGENCY**.

Eye injury. If severe it's an **EMERGENCY**.

Diseases. There are lots of them with some very strange names, so don't attempt to diagnose. Be vigilant and call your vet right away if you suspect any sort of severe illness. Here's a quick rundown of the most common maladies:

Bacterial diseases, such as Psittacosis and infections by Klebsiella, Pseudomonas and E.Coli.

• Psittacosis can be deadly if not treated early. Although diagnosis is often difficult, its flu-like symptoms may include ruffled feathers, poor appetite and weight loss, listlessness, eye and nasal discharge and loose green droppings. While common, tremors, convulsions and other signs of a misfiring central nervous system may also be present. Humans too can contract psittacosis; it feels like a cold or a mild flu and as a rule is no more serious.

Infections from fungal organisms such as Aspergillosis, an infection of the respiratory system. In cockatoos, Aspergillosis symptoms may include wheezing and labored breathing. While not fast to kill, the disease is debilitating and tenacious.

Infections from viral diseases such as Proventicular Dilatation, Polyomavirus and Psittacine Beak and Feather Disease.

• Polyomavirus affects mainly young birds and is fatal. The only sure cure is prevention: a two-shot vaccination series between 21 and 35 days of age. Dates of vaccination should appear on your sales contract.

• Cockatoos are particularly vulnerable to Psittacine Beak and Feather Disease, whose chief symptoms are deformed feathers and so-called "beak-rot." Because it depresses the

Table 5- Toxic Fumes
Asbestos
Bleach/chlorine
Carbon monoxide
Cigarette smoke
Diazanon
Duraflame logs
Flea bombs and collars
Floor polishes
Formaldehyde
Hair dye and spray
House paint (wet)
Kerosene
Matches
Moth balls
Nail polish and remover
Oil paint
Oven cleaner
Paint remover
Perfume
Pesticides
Shoe polish and cleaners
Spot removers
Spray starch
Suntan lotions
Surgical acrylics
Teflon surfaces (when heated)
Toilet cleaners
Wax

immune system it can kill either directly or via other infections. Young birds die quickly. Presently there is no cure or vaccination available in the United States.

Flu and colds. We've all heard of the dreaded avian flu, but unless your bird comes in close contact with wild birds or poultry the like-lihood of her getting it is close to nil. Birds are also susceptible to human-borne viruses, including some strains of flu and the common cold. If you're sick wash your hands extra-thoroughly before handling her and don't breathe directly on her; indeed, if you're really spewing out cold and flu bugs, cover your face with a surgical mask.

Infections from intestinal or blood parasites. If you adopted your bird from a reputable source parasites are unlikely. Again, though, if you suspect them consult your vet.

Drastic changes in feather coloring. Call your vet ASAP.

Severely overgrown beak. Used for eating, drinking, climbing and feeling as well as offense and defense--in sum, for sheer survival--a healthy beak is crucial.

85

Should it become so deformed or overgrown that it keeps her from eating she could quickly starve to death. While trimming her beak, your veterinarian will check for malocclusion,

Table 6- Household Poisons

Acetone	Iodine
Alcohol	Kerosene
Algae toxins	Lawn fertilizers
Ammonia	Lighter fluid
Amphetamines	Lye
Antifreeze	Matches (except safety matches)
Arsenic	Medicines
Aspirin	Mothballs
Antifreeze	Nail polish and remover
Bleach	Oven cleaner
Copper and brass cleaner	Paint
Corn and wart remover	Paint remover
Cosmetics	Paint thinner
Crayons	Perfume
Deodorants	Pine oil
Detergents	Rat and mouse poison
Disinfectants	Shellac
Drain cleaner	Shoe polish
Fabric softener	Sleeping pills
Fireworks	Snail bait
Floor/furniture polish	Strychnine
Floor/furniture wax	Suntan lotion
Garbage toxins	Toilet bowl cleaner
Gasoline	Wood preservatives
Glues and epoxies	
Hair dyes	
Herbicides	
Indelible markers	
Insecticides	

Table7- Toxic Plants	Christmas rose
Aloe	Chrysanthemum
Amaryllis	Cineraria
Andromeda japonica	Clematis
Apple (seed)	Cordatum
Apricot (pit)	Cornplant (dracaena)
Asparagus fern	Crown vetch
Autumn crocus	Cyclamen
Azalea	Daffodil
Avocado (fruit and pit)	Daisy
Baby doll ti	Daphne
Baby's breath	Dieffenbachia
Balsam pear	Dracena plam
Baneberry	Dragon tree
Bird-of-paradise	Elephant ear
Bittersweet	Emerald feather
Black locust	Fiddle-leaf fig
Blue-green algae	Flamingo plant
Boxwood	Foxglove
Buckeye	Fruit salad plant
Buckthorn	Geranium
Buddhist pine	Galdiola
Buttercup	Hawaiian ti
Caladium	Heavenly bamboo
Castor bean	Hemlock, poison
Ceriman	Hemlock, water
Cherry tree	Hibiscus
China doll	Holly
Chinese evergreen	Horse chestnut
Christmas cactus	Hurricane plant

Hydrangea

Impatiens

Indian turnip

Iris

Ivy, most varieties

Jerusalem cherry

Jimsonweed

Kalanchoe

Larkspur

Laurel, all varieties

Lily, all varieties

Lobelia

Marble queen

Marijuana

Mexican breadfruit

Mistletoe

Monkshood

Morning glory

Mother-in-law's tongue

Narcissus

Nephthytis

Nightshade (solanum)

Norfolk pine

Oleander

Onion

Peach (leaves and pit)

Pencil catus

Philodendron (all)

Plum (leaves and pit)

Plumosa fern

Poinsettia

Pothos (all)

Precatory bean

Primula

Privet

Rhododendron

Ribbon plant

Sago palm (cycas)

Schefflera

String-of-pearls/beads

Sweet Pea

Taro bine

Tobacco

Tomato (green)

Tomato plant

Tulip

Weeping fig

Yesterday/today/tomorrow plant

Yew (all)

malnutrition and internal health issues. Cracks, rapid growth or changes in beak coloration may also indicate beak and feather disease.

TAKING YOUR COCKATOO TO THE VETERINARIAN

Use a rigid pet carrier of adequate size. Cover the bottom with a towel. Set the carrier on the front passenger floor or strap it onto the front passenger seat.

For routine visits give your bird a treat and a toy or two to occupy her during the ride.

For emergencies remove water cups, perches and toys. Treat the patient gently and keep her warm and quiet, if necessary covering the carrier. Leave droppings in carrier for vet's perusal. Bring along your records (see Section 7, Forms, checklists and records) and any medicine she's taking.

POST-TREATMENT CARE

Once the veterinarian has diag-nosed and treated your bird, it's up to you to nurse her back to health. Here are some pointers:

• Follow the prescribed regimen to a T.

• Use a small cage, covering bottom with towels and low-ering perches for ease of motion.

• Place food and water close by and serve her favorite dishes to encourage eating.

• Keep her warm, around 75 to 85 degrees. Hot packs, heating pads, electric blankets, all are fine if the wires are towel-wrapped and hidden.

• Maintain peace and quiet and restrict handling.

• Medicate only as prescribed. For oral medication use a syringe with the needle removed.

89

6

Training Your Cockatoo

A bird's eye view -
Photo by Michael Fink

A BIRD'S-EYE VIEW

Cockatoos in the wild have con-specific companions (friends of a feather). It follows that a single bird in captivity needs human interaction to compensate. Without appropriate behavioral training this need may manifest itself as some combination of screaming, biting and feather-picking.

At your request (the notion of "command' is foreign to cocka-toos) the socialized bird should "step up" to your finger, arm or a stick/perch and stay without bit-ing; remain on a gym, climbing tree or stand for extended peri-ods; allow herself to be wrapped in a towel; and go to bed more or less peacefully. Patience, praise, reward, distraction and redirection are the only options for training her. Distraction is getting her attention off the fin-ger she's biting. Redirection is substituting a stick for the leg of the antique chair she's gnawing.

Punishment is at odds with her nature and will only cause or

91

Cirque de Soleil

worsen bad behavior. Consider also that ostensibly bad behavior may stem from a health problem or the onset of sexual maturity. It may even be a curtain that flutters oh so sinisterly when the furnace blower goes on. Stay alert: the solution may be right in front of you.

Above all train your bird to entertain herself. You can't just set her in front of the TV (though research along these lines, e.g., birdie TV, is currently underway).

B(ird)TV.

Most birds tune out non-interactive input such as television. So Alex trainer Dr. Irene Pepperberg and members of MIT's Media Lab are developing interactive alternatives. Like surfing the Web. Using a flat-panel liquid crystal monitor and a custom mouse, Dr. Pepperberg's African Grays can now waste their time just like us humans, if not (yet) at the same skill levels.

No, BTV is not available at your local electronics superstore. But stay tuned.

Maybe living indoors isn't so bad
Photo by Ginger Russell

The cockatoo who isn't having fun will find fun to have, which for you may be no fun at all.

RULES OF THE TRAINING GAME

You're not really training her, you know, you're persuading her to do you a favor. Be direct. Act calmly and confidently. Proceed as though you're in charge.

Heed her body language. If she's not in the mood forget it.

Keep her at a level slightly lower than your head. Height is a control issue with birds.

Train in a neutral room such as a hall or spare bedroom. Again, the main reason is control: it's like home field advantage. It also helps her focus. To further minimize distraction, close and cover all windows, shut all doors and remove or neutralize all hazards before starting.

Set boundaries. Teach your bird where her boundaries lie and make her stay within them. Start by controlling access to her cage. Don't let her traipse in and out at will; always ask her to "step up" when you take her out and "step down" when you put her in. On the other hand, don't be so restrictive that "boundaries" becomes a euphemism for jail. Play with her frequently outside the cage and provide an appropriate size gym or climb-ing tree--teaching her that these too have boundaries.

Never let her ignore a command (request). For cockatoos the exception fast becomes the rule.

Talk to her constantly, preferably in context so she can associate words with acts and objects.

Look her in the eye. Eye contact is as meaningful to your bird as it is to you. Trust, authority, approval, reprimand, each can be conveyed with a look. The "evil eye," for instance, tells her she's misbehaving and usually elicits an appropriate response. Avoiding eye contact is also meaningful, but in a negative sense; she'll likely interpret it as subservience (even little 'toos have big egos) and treat you accordingly.

Observe and interpret. This is especially important when it comes to behavior. Find the cause you'll likely find the cure. If she starts screaming at nine put her to bed at eight. If she plays atop the cage for 15 minutes and ventures off, put her back in the cage after ten or twelve minutes. And so forth.

Be realistic. As much as you like to think you understand her, and she you, there are limits. She, after all, is a bird, and you, after all, are not.

93

BASIC TRAINING

Step up. If your newly-weaned bird has been hand-fed and socialized she may already be a stepper-upper. If not, practice step-up and -down for five or so minutes several times a day. (Longer sessions cause what? Ah, yes, *boredom*.)

Mr. Terry and I

If she's gentle, press your hand (wrist, forearm) or a stick (dowel, perch, T-stand) against her breast and say step up in a firm but friendly voice. Parrots often use their beaks to help them climb so don't panic if her beak precedes her foot. No deal? Press just hard enough to threaten her balance. Still no deal? Place your other hand on her back and coax her forward. Alter technique and persist until you get results, then shower her with praise and give her a small treat, say a pumpkin or sunflower seed (save the peanut for last). Include hand to hand, hand to stationery perch, hand to hand-held perch and hand-held perch to hand-held perch.

94 Stepping down is generally easier. Place her in front of the training perch close enough to step onto it; then as you say step down tilt your hand/arm/stick forward (beak-first), forcing her to reach for the perch in order to keep her balance.

Toweling. A great way to restrain your bird for examinations, clippings, medical treatment and so forth, is to wrap her in a towel (size depends on the bird). If she hasn't been raised with towels you'll have to get her used to them. Not too fast, though, she's easily startled; and never from above, triggering her instinctive fear of hawks and such. Hold the towel in both hands and approach her slowly from the front, making eye contact if possible, as in "trust me." Play with her, covering her and then pulling the towel away with a big "Peekaboo!" Before long she'll lose all fear of Mr. Terry.

Stay. If she looks like she wants to fly, raise a hand and say firmly, *"Stay."* If she stays, reward her with a kind word and a scratch on the head, even a small treat once in a while. If she flies, put her back where she was and ignore her.

Repeat in short sessions until she gets the idea.

Gentleness ("No bite!"). Most cockatoos are docile yet sensitive. As a rule, biting is caused not by aggression but by anxiety--fear, control, territoriality ("What's *your* hand doing in *my* cage?") or, as in humans, redirected emotion ("I'm upset because Billy's been teasing me but since Billy's not around I'll bite you"). Always watch her body language and move slowly and deliberately.

When she bites *don't strike back*; you'll not only make things worse but also undermine her trust in you. Instead distract her. If she's perched on your hand drop the hand sharply (though not so sharply as to shake her off) or wave your free hand or say No! or kick a bucket, anything to divert her attention from whichever of your appendages she's feeding on. Then renew step-up training to re-establish your authority. Be gentle and patient: usually this too shall pass. If not, enlist the aid of a bird behaviorist. (See Section 3, Understanding your cockatoo.)

Potty training. Watch her until you have a good idea of when she poops and what body language (e.g., tail wag) precedes it. Then several times daily step her up, hold her over the chosen target (the sink, the toilet) and say "Launch torpedoes!" (Or whatever, so long as you're consistent.) Don't berate her if she potties by mistake; her rate of metabolism is steeper than her learning curve. In time she'll reward your patience and conform to pattern. Praise her when she does so until she does so by request instead of coincidence.

Speech training. Firstly, not all parrots talk, including many Amazons and African Grays, so consider it a real blessing if your cockatoo does. Also keep in view that 'toos have a hard time with consonants, so like Porky Pig yours may substitute W for R and the like. Because their voices are higher-pitched than those of Amazons and African Grays they generally respond better to female speech instructors.

Speech training requires patience, consistency, clarity of pronunciation and lots of encouragement and reward. Also bear in mind that your bird learns best in context. Name things as you offer them--ball, apple, dictionary--and praise her when she takes them, then do it again and again until she masters the word or phrase. As always, keep the lessons short (remember that child's attention span) and impart them in a quiet room. Recordings are okay, but if she

95

Get a cockatoo if you want to play
If you want to talk get an African Gray
*Left: Reprinted by permission
The Oasis Sanctuary
Right: Photo by Tom Trebisky*

learns to talk with no one around she may not talk when someone is.

Tricks. Most tricks are natural behaviors placed on queue. Bouncing, for example, or displaying the wings. Again, short sessions several times daily. Simple tricks include the above, plus bobbing the head, placing objects in a container, rolling over, and playing fetch (usually with you as the fetcher). More dexterous and nimble than New World parrots, cockatoos are better makers and users of tools, players of games and solvers of puzzles. Better comedians, too.

A hundred and fifty channels on TV. With a cockatoo who needs them?

The King's English

Like operating systems in new computers, human syntax – the basic pattern of all languages – comes pre-installed in every child. Vocabulary and such are programmed as the infant interrelates with other humans. But use it or lose it: after a window of roughly three years it is increasingly difficult for a child to acquire his first language. In effect his syntax Acrashes@ and he can't learn to combine words into meaningful sentences.

Similar rules may govern language acquisition in other animals. Only whales, dolphins, bats (yes, bats) and members of two bird orders-- Passeriformes (specifically the oscine songbirds) and Psittaciformes (parrots)--have consistently shown the ability to learn vocalizations (although some studies suggest that Trochiliformes, or hummingbirds, also possess this trait).

The best by far at human speech is the African Gray parrot. But if syntax is actually hard-wired, then even Alex, perhaps the most linguistically erudite of all the Grays, will never truly speak the King's English. Says Alex's trainer, Dr. Irene Pepperberg, "I avoid the language issue. I'm not making claims. His behavior gets more and more advanced, but I don't believe years from now you could interview him...What little syntax he has is very simplistic."

Cacatua galerita pictured in
Greensborough, Australia

Photo by Robert Tudor

Forms, Checklists, and Records

It's fun to hang from a street light
Photo by Andy Cranston

Adopter's checklist

What to look for when shopping for a cockatoo.

- ☐ Eyes
- ☐ Nasal openings
- ☐ Beak
- ☐ Wings and plumage
- ☐ Legs
- ☐ Feet
- ☐ Vent
- ☐ Droppings
- ☐ Behavior

Other issues

- ☐ The sales contract
- ☐ Quarantine certificate
- ☐ Sex determination
- ☐ Banding and microchip identification

Take-Home Shopping List

This is a reminder list of things to take home with your new cockatoo. You may think you don't need them all right away, but if forewarned is forearmed, forearmed is even better. Consult your retailer or breeder regarding the specific bird. The category "other" includes extra bowls and such as well as stuff the bird may not want or need but you really like.

Paperwork

- ☐ Signed contract (Breeder, Retailer, Owner)
- ☐ Quarantine certificate (if applicable)

Getting Ready

- ☐ Cage and accessories (perches, bowls, water bottle, etc.)
- ☐ Gym and accessories
- ☐ T-stand
- ☐ Sun lamp
- ☐ Cage cover
- ☐ Floor covering (chair mats, car pet protector)
- ☐ Spray bottles
- ☐ Poop-Off cleaning fluid
- ☐ Cockatoo shampoo
- ☐ Pellet and seed mix
- ☐ Cooked food mix (legumes and cereals)
- ☐ Treats
- ☐ Toys, toys, toys
- ☐ Air filter
- ☐ Humidifier
- ☐ Other

Maintenance Schedule

These are guidelines rather than hard-and-fast rules. Alter to fit your circumstances and the bird's needs/preferences

Instructions for Sitter or Boarding Facility

This form is designed for use by a professional bird sitter or specialized boarding facility. If instead you're leaving your bird with an inexperienced friend or relative, make sure he/she reads and understands this book and receives basic hands-on training for a few days prior to your departure.

Maintenance Schedule

Medical Examinations	
Initial	Within 30 days of purchase
Routine	Yearly
Vaccinations	
Polyomavirus series	Prior to taking bird home
Other	As needed
Weight check	Monthly
Grooming	
Claw trim	As needed
Wing trim	As needed
Bath	
Warm shower	Weekly
Hand spray bath	Daily
Hygiene	
Change cage liner	Daily
Clean dishes & bottles	Daily
Hand vacuum & spray-wash cage, gym, perches, etc.	Daily
Remove & clean soiled perches, toys, etc.	As needed
Scrub & sterilize cage, trays, gym, perches, etc.	Every few weeks
Feeding	
Pellet & seed mix	Free access; change daily
Cooked food (legume & cereal mix)	Mornings
Fruits & vegetables	Once or twice daily
Treats	As appropriate
Rotate toys	At least twice weekly
Provide interactive play time	At least 30 minutes daily

Instructions for Sitter or Boarding Facility

Bird
Name _____ Band # _____ Age _____ Species _____

Owner
Name _____ Telephone _____ Address_____

Owner's Dates of Departure & Return   _____/_____

Where owner can be contacted during absence:

Date: From/To   Address/Telephone

_____/_____   _____/_____

_____/_____   _____/_____

Veterinarian

Name _____ Telephone _____ Address _____

☐ Has permission to treat bird and charge to my account.

24/7 Emergency Facility

Name _____ Telephone _____ Address _____

Other contacts

Name _____ Telephone _____ Address _____

Name _____ Telephone _____ Address _____

Special Instructions

Favorite Toys _____

Food/Treats	Time	Comments
_____	_____	_____
_____	_____	_____

Leave in Cage   ☐ All the time   ☐ Only at night   ☐ Leave cage door open   ☐ Cover cage at night

Instructions regarding other pets _____

Behavioral quirks _____

Play & handling _____

Special precautions _____

This form is designed for use by a professional bird sitter or specialized boarding facility.

Yellow-crested cockatoo sitting on a streetlight in
Canberra, Australia

Photo by Andy Cranston

Veterinary Visit Checklist

Describe the main problem _____

_____

Provide a succinct chronological narrative of the illness _____

_____

Name of bird _____ Age _____ Sex _____ Species_____

How long have you had her? _____ Where did you acquire her? _____

Imported from _____ Quarantine certificate ☐ Yes ☐ No

Does she chew on things around the house? ☐ Yes ☐ No Specifically? _____

_____

Describe changes in her environment, food or routine _____

_____

Is she getting enough exercise? ☐ Yes ☐ No Companionship? ☐ Yes ☐ No Where's her cage located? _____

What kind of heating/cooling system do you have? _____

What other pets do you have? _____

Has any of them been ill of late? ☐ Yes ☐ No Describe illness _____

Have you or anyone in the household been ill of late? ☐ Yes ☐ No Describe illness _____

Do you wash your hands before handling the bird? ☐ Yes ☐ No

Describe the bird's diet (Morning)_____

(Afternoon)_____

(Evening) _____

How is the food stored? _____

Current medication and condition for which prescribed _____

_____

Describe allergies _____

Do you keep a record of illnesses and treatments? ☐ Yes ☐ No

Previous veterinarian _____ Telephone _____ Email _____

Comments _____

103

This form will help the veterinarian diagnose and treat your bird.
Be sure to take along other pertinent records as well.

Records

Initial Veterinary Examination

Date _____   Bird's Name _____   Age _____

Species _____   Band # _____

Veterinarian _____

Address _____

Telephone _____   Email Address _____

Weight _____   General Condition _____

_____

_____

_____

Test Results

    Gram Stain

    Feces _____   Choane _____

    Culture and Sensitivity _____

    CBC (Complete Blood Count) _____

    Psittacosis Test: Blood _____   Feces _____

    Fecal _____

    _____

    X-Rays _____

    _____

    _____

    Comments _____

    _____

    _____

Past health problems often bear on future health problems.
Consequently, the more complete your bird's records the better her veterinarian
will be able to diagnose and treat her.

Records

Subsequent Veterinary Examinations

Date _____   Bird's Name _____   Age _____

Veterinarian _____Telephone _____Fax _____

Weight _____   General Condition _____

Diagnostic Procedures	Date	Results
Cultures _____	_____	_____
Blood tests _____	_____	_____
Electrocardiograms _____	_____	_____
X-Rays _____	_____	_____
Endoscopy _____	_____	_____
Biopsy _____	_____	_____
Cytology _____	_____	_____
Urinalysis _____	_____	_____
Fecal _____	_____	_____

Treatment _____

_____

Surgery

Date _____   Type _____

Results _____

_____

_____

Treatment _____

_____

_____

Comments _____

Records

Illnesses & Injuries

Date _____   Bird's Name _____   Age _____

Type of Illness/Injury _____

_____

_____

_____

Treatment

    Attending Veterinarian _____

    Treatment _____

    _____

    _____

    _____

    ☐ At Home   ☐ Veterinarian Consulted

    Treatment _____

    _____

    _____

    _____

    Medication and dosage (be specific) _____

    _____

    _____

    _____

    Resolution _____

    _____

    _____

    _____

Important Telephone Numbers & Addresses

Veterinarian _____Telephone_____After Hours _____

Fax _____Email Address _____Website _____

Address _____

☐ Retailer   ☐ Breeder   ☐ Former Owner

Address _____

Telephone _____ Email Address_____

Bird Behaviorist _____

Address _____

Telephone _____ Email Address _____

Emergency Clinic or Vet. Hospital _____

Address _____

Telephone _____ Email Address _____

Poison Control Center _____

Address _____

Telephone _____ Email Address _____

Bird Sitter _____

Address _____

Telephone _____ Email Address _____

ASPCA (American Society for the Prevention of Cruelty to Animals)

Address _____

Telephone _____ Email Address _____

Local Bird Club _____

Contact Name(s) _____

Address _____

Telephone _____ Email Address _____

Other _____

Contact Name(s) _____

Address _____

Telephone _____ Email Address _____

Important telephone numbers and addresses

Appendix

"G'day, mate! I'm a kookaburra, but some of
my best friends are cockatoos"
Photo by Robert Tudor

GEOGRAPHICAL DISTRIBUTION OF COCKATOOS

Ranging north to south from the Philippines to Tasmania, cockatoos are native to the island rainforests of Indonesia and to the coastal forests, grasslands, deserts and wastelands of Australia. (See map.)

Their habitat, especially in Australia, continues to be decimated by timber barons, mining companies, farmers, land developers et al under the aegis of short-sighted and/or self-seeking economic policy makers.

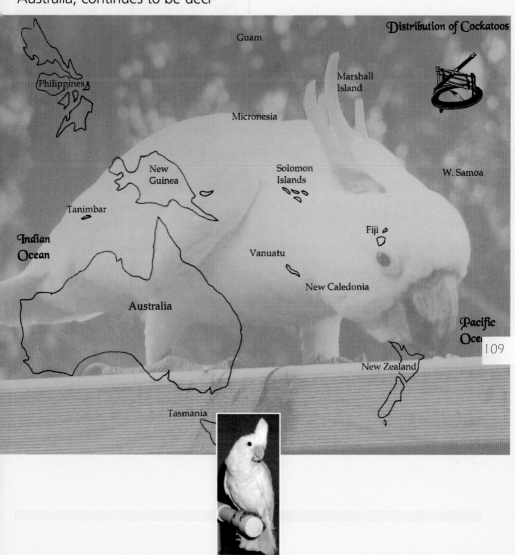

Distribution of Cockatoos

Guam

Marshall Island

Philippines

Micronesia

New Guinea

Solomon Islands

W. Samoa

Tanimbar

Indian Ocean

Fiji

Vanuatu

Australia

New Caledonia

Pacific Ocean

New Zealand

Tasmania

TAXONOMY OF COCKATOOS

Parrots form their own order, Psittaciformes, which in turn comprises two families: Cacatuidae (cockatoos and cockatiels) and Psittacidae (parrots, parakeets, conures, macaws and lories). Some experts split off the nectar-eating lories and lorikeets into a separate family called Loriidae. Cacatuidae trace back more than forty million years to northwest Queensland, Australia.

Biological Classification of Cockatoos

(among experts classifications may differ)

Kingdom - Animalia

Phylum - Chordata
(fishes, amphibians, reptiles, birds, mammals)

Subphylum - Vertebrata

Class - Aves (birds)

Order - Psittaciformes
(parrots and allies)

Family - Cacatuidae (cockatoos)

Subfamily - Cacatuinae
110 (true cockatoos)

Genus - Probosciger

Species - Palm

Palm cockatoo.

Rare and very expensive, this largest and most spectacular of cockatoos has a large beak built like a ratcheted nutcracker, capable of cracking Brazil nuts and even the rock-hard shell of the Pandanus palm nut, its favorite delicacy. Good tempered, but too big for a cage. Habitat, rainforests of New Guinea and Australia's Cape York Peninsula
Photo by Everett Butler

Genus - Calyptoihynchus
Species -
Red-tailed black or Banksian
Glossy black
Funereal or yellow-tailed
White-tailed black or Baudin's

Genus - Callocephalon

Species - Gang-gang or red-crowned or helmeted

Genus - Eolophus

Species -
Red-breasted or
Roseate or Galah

Genus - Cacatua

Species
Phillipine or red-vented
Goffin's
Bare-eyed or Little Corella
Slender-billed
Ducorp's
Blue-eyed

Gang-gang cockatoo.

Rare in captivity. Expensive. Good talkers but highly active, aggressive and prone to feather picking when caged. Habitat, mountain forests of southeastern Australia to northern Tasmania

Photo by Andy Cranston

Slender-billed cockatoo.

Moderately rare. Aggressive. Expensive. Long bill designed for uprooting bulbs and roots and digging tunnels. Generally unsuited for the cage. Habitat, wooded grasslands and savannas of southeastern Australia

Photo by Feathered Follies

111

Blue-eyed cockatoo.

Closely related to Galerita and similarly tempered. Moderately rare. Expensive. Habitat, forested islands off eastern New Guinea, especially New Ireland and New Britain

Photo by Everett Butler

Greater Sulphur-crested

Lesser Sulphur-crested

Umbrella-crested,

White-crested or Greater White-crested

Moluccan

Leadbeater or Major Mitchell's

Major Mitchell's Cockatoo.

Beautiful but rare. Aggressive. Expensive. Generally unsuited for the cage. Habitat, shrublands of central and southwestern Australia

Photo by Feathered Follies

Color Classification of Cockatoos

Umbrella, all white, crest included

Umbrella Cockatoo (C. alba)

Sulphur-crested, all white, yellow crest, greater in size

Greater Sulphur-Crested (C. galerita galerita)

Eleonora (C. galerita eleonora)

Fitzroy Greater Sulphur-Crested (C. galerita fitzroyi)

Triton (C. galerita triton)

Sulphur-crested, all white, yellow or yellow-orange crest, smaller in size

Lesser Sulphur-Crested (C. sulphurea sulphurea)

Abbott's Lesser Sulphur-Crested (C. sulphurea abbotti)

Citron-Crested (C. sulphurea citrinocristata)

Djampeana Lesser Sulphur-Crested
(C. suplhurea djampeana)

Occidental Lesser Sulphur-Crested
(C. sulphurea occidentalis)

Little-Billed Lesser Sulphur-Crested
Cockatoo (C. sulphurea parvula)

Blue-eyed, white body, yellow crest

Blue-Eyed (C. ophthalmica)

*Smaller whites, small white crests,
other identifying features*

Goffin's (C. goffini)

Bare-Eyed
(C. sanguinea sanguinea)

Little Bare-Eyed
(C. sanguinea normantoni)

Slender-Billed
(C. tenuirostris tenuirostris)

Southwestern Slender-Billed
(C. tenuirostris pastinator)

Red-Vented (C. haematuropygia)

Ducorp's (C. ducorps)

*White body plumage, pastel pink all
over, darker red crests*

Leadbeater or Major Mitchell's
(C. leadbeateri leadbeateri)

Molly's Leadbeater
(C. leadbeateri mollis)

Moluccan (C. moluccensis)

*Black cockatoos range from gray to
black; some feathers may be edged
in pink or red*

Charcoal black with bare red face

Black Palm
(Probosciger aterrimus)

Probosciger aterrimus goliath
(Probosciger aterrimus
stenolophus)

Black with varying tail colors

Yellow-Tailed Black
(Calyptorhynchus funereus
funereus)

White-Tailed Black Cockatoo
(Clyptorhynchus funereus
baudinii)

Glossy
(Calyptorhynchus lathami)

Red-tailed Black
(Calyptorhynchus magnificus)

*Gray with red head on male, red
breast shadings on female*

Gang-Gang
(Callocephalon fimbriatum)

*Gray about the back, wings and
tail, but with pink or rose color on
the entire breast*

Rose-Breasted or Galah
(Eolophus roseicapillus)

113

ASSOCIATIONS & RESCUE ORGANIZATIONS

Association of Avian Veterinarians
P.O. Box 811720
Boca Raton FL 33481
Tel: (561)393-8901
Website: www.aav.org

American Federation of Aviculture
P.O. Box 91717
Austin TX 78709-1717
Tel. 512-585-9800
Website: http://www.afabirds.org
Email: afaoffice@earthlink.net

The Gabriel Foundation
1025 Acoma Street
Dever, CO 80204
Tel: (303) 629-5900
Website: thegabrielfoundation.org
Email: gabriel@thegabrielfounda-tion.org

Kaytee Avian Foundation - Adopt-an-Acre
P.O. Box 230
Chilton WI 53014
Tel: 800-KAYTEE1
Website: kaytee.com
Click on Avian Foundation

Midwest Avian Research Expo
1599 Genesee Road
E Concord NY 14055-9607
Tel: 800-453-5833

PEAC
Parrot Education & Adoption Center
P.O. Box 600423
San Diego CA 92160-0423
Tel: 619-287-8200
Website: peac.org
Email: parroted@cox.net

RARE Center for Tropical Conservation
1840 Wilson Blvd., Suite 402
Arlington VA 22201-3000
Tel: 703-522-5070
Website: rarecenter.org

World Parrot Trust USA
P.O. Box 935
Lake Alfred, FL 33850
Tel: 863-956-4347
Website: worldparrottrust.org
Email: usa@worldparrottrust.org

Bird Placement Program
P.O. Box 183
Medina, Ohio 44258-0183
Website: avi-sci.com/bpp/

Foster Parrots Ltd.
P.O. Box 650
Rockland MA 02370
Tel: 781-878-3733
Website: fosterparrots.com

Oasis Sanctuary Foundation Ltd.
P.O. Box 30502
Phoenix, AZ 85046-0502
Tel: 520-212-4737
Website: the-oasis.org
Email: oasis@the-oasis.org

The Tropics Exotic Bird Refuge
P.O. Box 686
Kannapolis NC 28082-0686
Tel: 704-932-8041
Website: tropics.parrotrefuge.com
Email: tropics@juno.com

FURTHER READING

Periodicals
Bird Talk
P.O. Box 6050
Mission Viejo CA 92690
Website:
www.birdtalkmagazine.com

Companion Parrot Quarterly
239 E 4th Street
Loveland CO 80537
Tel: 970-278-0233
Website: companionparrot.com
Email:
staff@companionparrot.com

Books
Athan, Mattie Sue. *Guide to Companion Parrot Behavior.* Haupauge NY: Barron's, 1999.

Barber, Theodore X, Ph.D. *The Human Nature of Birds.* Northwestern University Press, 2000

Burger, Joanna. *The Parrot Who Owns Me.* New York: Random House, 8 2001.

Diefenbach, Karl. *The World of Cockatoos.* Trans. Annemarie Lambrich. Neptune City NJ: T.F.H. Publications, 1985

Jupiter, Tony and Mike Parr. *Parrots: A Guide to Parrots of the World.* New Haven CT: Yale University Press, 1998

McWatters, Alicia. *A Guide to a Naturally Healthy Bird.* East Canaan CT: Safe Goods, 1997.

Murphy, James J. *Cockatoos Are Different Because They Have Crests.* Gilbert PA: White Mountain Bird Farm, 1998.

Spadafori, Gina and Brian L. Speer. *Birds for Dummies*. Foster City CA: IDG Books Worldwide, 1999.

Avian Publications
6380 Monroe Street, NE
MN 55432
www.avianpublications.com

ILLUSTRATIONS

The Authors neither make, offer nor afford any rights to the illustrations of this book; they are owned by the Illustrators and used with permission.

Development of Umbrella Cockatoos Page 76

> *Illustrations by*
> *Karen McGovern,*
> *Rare Species Conservatory*
> *Foundation,*
> *www.rarespecies.org,*
>
> *reprinted by permission*

Dinosaur Page 13, Kung Fu Page 72, Digestive System Page 78 and Skeletal System Page 77

> *Illustrations by*
> *Natalie Love Adams,*
> *Atalina's Creations,*
> *atalinas@gmail.com*

PHOTOGRAPHS

Thanks to the many photographers around the world that help capture the lovable personality of the cockatoo.

Australia

Dey Alexander,
Cheltenham VIC Australia,
email: dey.personal@gmail.com

> Pages: 58, Cover

Andy Cranston,
Canberra ATC Australia,
email: andy.cranston@gmail.com

> Pages: 22, 47, 49, 98, 102, 111

Roberta Tudor,
Greensborough VIC Australia,
website:
www.thetudors.net/LocalBirds.htm

> Pages: 10, 39, 45, 49, 97, 108

Cover Photo Credit

USA

Laurie Baker, Owner
& *Jeanni Landry*, Manager,
Feathered Follies, Lafayette, CA,
www.feathered-follies.com
Email: feathered@sbcglobal.net

> Pages: 15-17, 28, 40, 42, 46, 55, 59, 67, 68, 73, 81, 111, 112

Everett Butler, Woodburn Oregon,
email: butlereverett@aol.com

> Pages: 24-27, 55, 57, 61, 110, 112, Cover

Elizabeth Cantu,
Feather Fu, Austin Texas,
Replacement Strategy Toys
www.featherfu.com

> Page 82, photo (1)

Michael Fink,
Phoenix, AZ,
website: www.micktravels.com
email: mick@micktravels.com

> Page 5, 21, 27, 29, 90

Charlotte Fox,
Office Manager,
The Oasis Sanctuary
Sponsored birds at The Oasis,
Phoenix, AZ
website: www. the-oasis.org
email: off.mgr@the-oasis.org

Pages: 75, 96

Stacey Hoth,
Training Director,
A Refuge for Saving Wildlife, Inc.,
Northbrook, Illinois
website: www.rescuethebirds.org
emial: info@rescuethebirds.org.

RSW is a not-for-profit parrot rescue,
rehabilitation, education, & adoption,
no-kill shelter facility. They are
accredited by the Association of
Avian Rescue Organizations (AARO),
certified by the Model Aviculture
Program (MAP), licensed by the
Illinois Department of Agriculture,
Bureau of Animal Welfare. They are
also a member of the Society of
Animal Welfare Administrators.

Page: 24 (Headshot of Koko, a
female Umbrella Cockatoo who
came to the Refuge a very scared
and emotionally wrecked bird. She
went to live with Robyn one of the
volunteers at the Refuge.

Ginger Russell,
Roswell NM
Marketing on Demand
email: marketingondemand@q.com

Pages: 4, 7-9, 12, 16, 19, 23, 35,
37, 42, 50-53, 63, 64, 66, 75, 82,
91, 92, 94, Cover

Tom Trebisky,
Webmaster,
The Oasis Sanctuary,
Phoenix AZ
Sponsored birds at The Oasis
website: www. the-oasis.org
Page: 96, Photo (2)

117

Hey, what am I doing in a cockatoo book!
Kookaburras, native to Australia
Photo by Patrick Durrell

A mess of cockatoos in their native land of Australia
Photo by Patrick Durrell

Yellow-crested cockatoo
sitting on a streetlight
in Canberra,
Australia.

Photo by Andy Cranston

Max grew his feathers back due
Photo by

120

Hello Cocky, Yellow-crested cockatoo pictured in Cheltenham, Australia
Photo by Dey Alexander

Bare-eyed Cockatoo.
Photo by Feathered Follies

Coco, Goffin's Cockatoo.
Photo by Ginger Russell

Coco, Enjoys art too!
Photo by Ginger Russell

Index

Index